The
Diary of A
Saved
Black Woman

By Pamela C Mason

Like a swimmer entering the pool, little by little I immerse myself into life's cool water. I stop every now and then to adjust to the temperature, then press forward a step or two with the goal of eventually being able to swim freely. Some would rather dive in, but many of us cannot handle the sudden shock; for me, it is a lifetime of gradual adaptations.

1999

Milestones

Introduction

Because of their years in slavery, the Israelites no longer knew what freedom meant, and they forgot that their purpose, as a nation, was to show the world God's character through their lives. God told Pharaoh, "Let my people go!" Go where? Why did it take so long? How could God's chosen people be lost, traveling with Him right there in their midst?

Like many stories in the Bible, the story of the Exodus from Egypt is not just a history lesson; it is rich with object lessons for our life's journey.

> I knew things had to change; I just wasn't sure how. I had dreams of peace and tranquility. Life was getting way too scary and the people I had come to rely on were becoming unpredictable and fear-provoking. There is an old saying, "Better, the devil you KNOW." Was this my destiny?

> I did not want to leave that which had become familiar and comfortable, but I knew God had much more for me and mine. I had to prepare to stand on the only firm foundation, the only SURE thing I knew— God had the plan. Was I ready to walk, in blind faith, into my "Land of Promise"?

The following journal is the story of how God took a fearful scrawny character and developed a mighty warrior of faith.

In some instances, it may seem that small events are taken way too seriously. I often mention them because God used those smaller actions to prepare me for the footmen and horsemen yet to come. Jer. 12:5

Like you did for Elisha and his servant: When horsemen are seemingly on my horizon, please open my eyes and let me see the angels of God that encircle me. II Kings 6:16-17

Note to the reader:

If a story seems to move too slowly and the indented paragraphs (of details) weigh you down, feel free to skip down to the next un-indented portion; but realize, often the axiom is in the details!

Furthermore, while you are welcome to check each Bible verse provided, that is not their purpose. I have, simply, provided the *source* of my thinking for anyone that may wonder about some of my points. This journey is not intended to be tedious; but it may sometimes make you climb!

A JOURNEY STARTED: (1984)

As I approach my thirties:

"They" say that most people don't have a clue about how life really works until they reach their thirties. Up to that point, you are too busy trying to prove your parents wrong. All of a sudden, somewhere around age thirty-five, your parents become wiser, and you hear their words coming out of your mouths.

I wonder …

Journey to Canaan

Exod. 3:7-8; 13:18, 21-22

The story of the Israelites' Exodus from Egypt has always intrigued me. Recognizing the many ways God beckoned, protected, provided for, and sustained them always served as an example of his loving faithfulness. Therefore, it was no wonder, during the lowest point in my life, that God used this treasure chest of analogical gems to teach me how to "step out in faith".

‍ஐ ON YOUR MARK ℭ

1984

For a couple of years or so, I felt as if I was sitting and waiting for something to happen. I could not figure out what or how. All I knew was that I was waiting. In time, I noticed stresses around me begin to escalate. I was trying to express my spiritual uneasiness to a friend when I said, "I feel like I'm sitting by the Red Sea." With that revelation came a wealth of understanding that unfolded, little by little, over the next several years.

The first gem the Lord revealed was "Be still and know that I am God." That started me in the path of studying. Whenever HE spoke, I needed to be able to react in confidence that it was God's voice and not MY wishes. I did not want to be deceived. I wanted to KNOW His voice. So, there I sat beside my *Red Sea* with trouble behind, impossibilities to the left and right, and afraid to go forward. Believe it or not, I was there about three years. Was I bored? Not in the least. The Lord set me to work. First the Lord had me learn of Him, then learn myself.

Remember, the twofold mission He gave me was: "<u>BE STILL</u> and <u>KNOW that I AM GOD</u>."

Let me share a little of the beauty I learned in the *Be Still* phase of this journey. Whenever a *storm* would start to brew, just like any good *Mother Hen*, I gathered my chicks beneath my wings and ran for shelter. For me, running for shelter meant doing busy work and activities that soothed the superficial problem, yet presented no real solution. Being still was a hard lesson for me. I ran from *shelter* to *shelter* so many times that running became second nature. But God was telling me to BE STILL. Frequently, I would find myself running up and down *the bank* looking over my shoulder and crying, "The *Egyptians* are coming!" But each time the Lord beckoned (oftentimes loudly; now and then in a whisper), "*Be Still* and KNOW that I am God."

Sometimes, with a tinge of humor, I prayed, "Lord You don't have to bother to open the water—just send a boat."

He replied, "Be still."
At times, I found some *twig* to *whittle*. Twigs were activities that kept my hands busy and mind on heaven, like ceramics and other arts and crafts.

Whittling allowed me to burn nervous energy while trying to be still. But eventually, God always longingly beckoned, "Settle down; be STILL." Mind you, I usually found good "reasons" for my activity. Sometimes, it was even noble activity, but the Lord had told ME to *Be Still*. Like a parent with a child filled with anticipation, the night before a birthday party, the Lord in His majestic patience would smile, look at me, and say, "Peace! Be Still."

During the *day* times, I noticed the *cloud of smoke* set between my Egyptians and me. During the *night's* darkness, there sat a fire of hope that shined bright. It was then, in the darkness of that despair, that I recognized God's omnipresence (or should I say *OMNIPRESENTS*). There was nothing that could reach me without His consent. It was then my Heavenly Father became my Heavenly Daddy. I rested in His arms and safely BEcame STILL; KNOWing Him as GOD!

ℰℴ GET SET ℭℛ

1985

I realized there was a journey ahead; the inspiration of preparation had taken over. There was no thing (and no one) that could stop me. I was truly stepping out on faith. I went back to school, found a job, and bought a car. I did not even know which state to register the car in. I didn't know where God was sending me—if He was sending me anywhere.

ℰℴ READY? ℭℛ

December 1986

It is baffling the people around me when they can see so much preparation. I still cannot explain what my plans are. I have none! The Lord has simply told me to prepare, nothing more. I am sure of one thing: whatever the Lord is preparing for me is more than I am used to handling. I guess He wants me to sharpen my skills because a *dull axe cannot clear the forests that lie ahead.*

ဆ GO! os

February 1987

During prayer in Divine Worship Service, I heard a voice within calling over my right shoulder. I looked up, in my mind, to my right and saw a wall of water. This somewhat startled me. I looked up, still in my mind, to my left. With a flinch, I saw another wall of water. I looked behind me and saw a long DIRT road. In front of me, another even longer dirt road. All of a sudden, it dawned on me –I had started across. The Lord had parted the *waters* and I was on DRY land. Just as suddenly, I heard that same voice speak to me, "Now is the time to decide. Do you want to go across or go back? I will be with you whichever way you go." The voice continued, "Realize, though, it is not Canaan you will reach on the other side of this river. It is the wilderness. I will be with you all the way, either way."

I prayed, "I don't want the flesh pots and I've come too far to start going backwards now. Lord, help me pass the snakes and the traps of the desert. I want to go forward!"

I praise the wonderful God we serve. Although I had been praying for YEARS to *cross*, He did not let me go blindly into the wilderness. He did not let me think, not even for a moment, that I would be alone.

By no means am I saying the travel will be easy. Already, like the Israelites there have been times when I found myself remembering *Egypt* and wondering if I made the right decision. I have to say though, I would rather die in the wilderness than be a *slave in Egypt.* God has been wonderful to me. As I continue to travel, I have become very determined that the journey is not in vain.

The Lord is steadfast:

Like *manna*: He has been my daily sustenance.

Like *water from a rock*: He has provided life-sustaining provisions from seemingly impossible sources.

Like the *pheasants*: Sometimes when I prayed for things that weren't the best for me, even though it pained Him to see me suffer, if I insisted, God in his infinite wisdom let me learn the hard way.

I pray that I, like Caleb, can withstand the temptation of intimidation. Num. 13:27-30

Where others see *GIANTS*,

may I see only the opportunity for the LORD

to be Glorified!

Even Dogs Get to Eat the Crumbs

Matt 15:26-27

A trilogy that got this *cat* to understand *dogs.*

King of the house!

1987

My sons and I spent a couple of months living at my sister Elena's house. That is when I came to realize that BIG dogs just need to be understood.

Elena has a dog name *King.* He is about three feet tall with all four paws on the ground and, therefore, meets you eye-to-eye when you sit on her couch. He is a Rottweiler/Doberman Pincher mix. When you first meet him, he seems to fit his name because his appearance intimidates you so. Even after visiting my sister for several family gatherings, I still kept a close watch on King, out of the corner of my eye, as we moved around the house. After actually living with them for a couple of months, I got to know the *real* King. He was nothing but a BIG spoiled puppy.

We laughed for days as King worked through his jealousy. At first, he followed me around the house keeping an eye on me. If I entered a room that he thought I should not be in, he would run to Elena and, in a method that I can only describe to the *Lassie Generation,* he would *tell on me.* It got to be very funny watching King tattletale every time Elena returned home; we treated it like a game of charades. Sometimes, I tried to do something difficult for him to convey, but somehow, some way, he always got the message across that I had been a *bad girl* AND exactly WHAT I had done.

This went on for weeks. You may think this would have driven us crazy, but in fact, it was a lot of fun watching him communicate SO clearly. In all his messages though, there was one message he *spoke* to me daily, and there was never to be any doubt what his message was. He *said,* "Remember, you are only here temporarily. Do not get too comfortable." King had no shame in his game! He made sure I knew my stay was to be temporary.

Don't we wish we could be so bold? Have you ever had a guest you wanted to tell to GO HOME!?

Well, sometime during the third or fourth week we were there, King got out. Actually, he just WALKED out the front door past my young sons. They did not have any hope in holding him back. Together they could have ridden on his back, and he still probably would have kept going. Elena was not at home, and I had to go get him. Lucky for me, he did not find it necessary to run since he was in complete control of the situation. Therefore, it was rather easy to follow him around the neighborhood. Finally, after several blocks, he stopped to nose around in a backyard, and I was able (no, HE ALLOWED me) to put the leash on him and return home. When we got back, I was so happy with him that I gave him several treats, told him how pleased I was with him, and how much of a GOOOD boy he was, all because he had come home so easily. That day, when Elena got home, I told her all about our adventure and how GOOOD King had been. King just loved all the attention. From that day on, King accepted me. We no longer got the daily updates. I was even allowed to enter any room in the house.

One night, I had a visitor. It was a person whose presence made me uncomfortable; Elena had given him entrance without asking me first. I felt certain that King would be there to protect me, so I agreed to sit in the living room and talk. As we sat talking, King slumped over and fell asleep against my leg. I thought to myself, *Wow, what kind of protection are you?*

Things went okay, and the conversation ended nicely, but I was truly disappointed in Kings lethargic style of protection.

The next morning, when Elena and I spoke about King's behavior, she told me that King was, indeed, sensing danger; otherwise, he would have left my side and stretched out in the middle of the room, as usual. Instead, he had positioned himself between the two of us. I then realized, from that awkward position, King could have quickly reacted to any sudden moves towards me. Even now, remembering the situation, I realize that his quiet presence had handled things.

Later that morning, King insisted on licking my toes (YUCK). Elena told me that that was his way of accepting me into the home. For the next couple of weeks, I got to see what a real friend King could be. I know for a fact that the experience of meeting King gave me a new outlook on dogs!

The Master Is Calling, Today!

In the spring of 1987, the boys and I moved into a beautiful home the Lord had prepared for us. By July or so, we started noticing problems in the neighborhood that made me give the idea of buying a dog a long hard thought. The boys had wanted one for a while. I figured it may be wise to get one now, to help us feel more secure.

After deciding, to get a puppy, we went to several animal shelters, which in itself became a real adventure. For several reasons I will not get into, we decided to look for a FEMALE puppy. We looked at everything from terriers to St. Bernards. We took them each on a LEASH (which, mine you, is the law) and tested their reactions to us as their masters. We finally came across the sweetest Rottweiler/German-Shepherd puppy. A rather BIG puppy, but still, nonetheless, a puppy. Her name was Nikki, and she was ready and willing to do whatever it took to please her new MASTERS.

When we got her home, we spent the next few days teaching her to follow basic commands like SIT, COME, DOWN, and NO. In her zeal to please us, she mastered these quickly and was ready to buckle down and concentrate on the more complex lessons. These could be considered more like rules than tricks that allowed us to coexist. They defined her purpose in the household. She, a dog, being the best dog she could be, could still be no more than a dog in her masters' house. Hence, the rules were there to keep her to the highest standard she, a dog, could be expected to achieve.

She was:

    (1)   Allowed in certain areas of the house but not in others.

    (2)   Allowed to relieve herself in a specific area of the yard.

    (3)   Allowed to chew only HER toys.

    (4)   Allowed to jump up on the boys; not me.

(5) Banned from flower beds, gardens, and compose heap.

(6) Forbidden to sit on the furniture.

(7) Forbidden to beg.

(8) Required to get in her *"PLACE"* when commanded.

(9) Expected to keep all strangers OUT, unless escorted in by one of her masters.

(10) Expected to protect her masters.

Each of them was essential, none greater than the other.

> For a while, it seemed as if there was always a NO attached to Nikki's name: NO Nikki for this; NO Nikki for that. However, once she learned the JOY in obedience, she soon settled into her niche in the family and seemed to love to hear, "GOOOD Girl!"

There is one trick, not mentioned as of yet, that many friends find quite captivating. Because I did not want scratch marks on the outside door, I hung a bell from the doorknob. At first, every time we took her out, we hit the bell to make it ring. After a week or so, we made her ring the bell by hitting it gently against her nose. After another week or so, we stood by the door until she rang the bell. Even now, we do not acknowledge her gyrations. She knows to ring the bell if she wants to go out.

Our house, an older house, has many doors and passageways that regulate the temperature by controlling the airflow. In the winter we keep the rooms warm by keeping all the doors shut. This presented a problem for Nikki. Using the bell trick, we strategically placed bells on the doors through which she traveled. The bells enable her to move throughout the house, as we allow her. She would *ring the bells* and then wait for one of us (her masters) to open the door.

For exercise, we try to take Nikki out regularly for walks around the neighborhood. We realize that lying around her masters' house, while quite comfy, makes a fat lazy dog. So, we do try to exercise her as much as we can. We started off using a leash (which is the law) and a choke chain. We thought the pull of the choke chain would settle her into *walking* instead of pulling. WRONG! The combination of her strength and foolishness was detrimental. Every time something interesting caught her eye, she would almost choke herself trying to go after it. In her quest for the shiny bauble, she did not realize how tight the choke-chain became around her neck. We very quickly bought her a *harness* and a short sturdy *leash*. This allowed us to control her without her harming herself.

As we walked the neighborhood, every now and then a cat crossed our path. Nikki, as you would expect any Dog (that is dog with a capital D) to do gives it her best shot to chase after it. Her *leap into action* is promptly followed by the command "SIT!" Then a lecture going something like this:

Don't forget yourself! Who's holding this leash? That's right! And I do not chase around the neighborhood after cats; therefore, NEITHER WILL YOU!

After which, we continue our walk.

Getting back to the yard Nikki looks forward to her reward for a good walk. *"Goood Girl!"* Then, off she goes, running and playing in the back yard, proud that she has pleased her master.

We've had Nikki almost a year now, and she has become part of the family. Not too long ago, we noticed that she was usually asleep when we got home. Often, she gave us a sleepy look from her bed as we walked through the family room. The look was one that said, *Oh, you're home.* We didn't think much of this, other than the fact that we felt a little taken for granted, until recently when the house got broken into. The police could tell that the burglars had been searching in the house for hours. We could not figure how this could be, considering the fact that Nikki lets NO ONE in the house. She was going ballistic with the police in the house. Finally, we figured it out. Nikki had been ASLEEP, and the burglars overcame her in some way.

After that, I installed an alarm system. It did not call anyone; I just wanted to *WAKE THE DOG.* We trained her to meet us at the door by giving her a treat when she responded to the beep. Now, when Nikki hears the beep from the alarm system, she runs down the steps to greet whichever master may have arrived. The thought being, *since she is eagerly awaiting her masters' return, she is additionally alert to anyone trying to sneak in.*

A few weeks ago, I woke with a thought on my mind: *Why do dogs always try to get out of the backyard? They have all the food they can eat given to them free of charge. Their loving masters provide their care. They do not have to worry about shelter. The only thing awaiting them outside of the yard is the unknown. They must worry about getting hit by cars. They revert to their untamed nature and hunt for food. They quickly become diseased and sickly. Their joy is gone because their only true joy comes from pleasing their master.*

The *floodgates* opened as God reminded me, *How true the Bible is, "As a dog returneth to its vomit; so a fool returneth to his folly."* Proverbs 26:11

I asked myself, *Why do WE spend so much time trying to escape from OUR Masters yard?* Then noted, We, like dogs, do not recognize the FREEDOM, inside the fence. Every morning for a week, I woke with Nikki on my mind and a new way of seeing myself:

I, like Nikki, was lost in a pound. My Master came and took me out of my cage to see if I would accept Him. He came and adopted me into His family. He took me, into His house, and gave me the responsibility of guarding His principles and precepts. He taught me:

SIT   *Be still and know that I am God* Ps. 46:10

I learned to sit, prepare, and wait on His call to action.

DOWN *He MAKETH me lie down in green pastures.*
                                                        Ps. 23:2

I learned that there are times He makes me *eat and rest* although I may not feel like it. Like the good shepherd, God knows life's journey. He knows when I need to graze in the present pasture. He even MAKES me rest. He knows the rough terrain ahead. He prepareth my soul!

COME *Who knoweth whether thou art come to the Kingdom for such a time as this?* Esther 4:14

Sometimes God calls us to a position to stand for Him. He may be calling us to do something way more than we believe we can achieve, but God has a plan. He reveals it in His own time. The key is to stay in tune with the Master's Call.

NO   Remember ... *No good thing shall I withhold*
                                                        Ps. 84:11

When God says no, we seldom WANT to hear it. It is usually because we have our own agenda, have left God's will, and have wandered off. When we hear that sharp NO, we must remember God has the whole picture in view.

God also gave me some rules to allow me to exist in His house: *The Ten Commandments* Exod. 20: 1-17

> I, a finite mortal, being the best I could be; could still be no more than a finite mortal in my Master's house. Hence, the rules are there to keep me to the highest standards I, a finite mortal, can be expected to achieve.

As I buckled down and got settled into these rules, my Master taught me a new trick.

When I reach a closed door before me, I could just ring the bell of FAITH and wait for my Master to come and open.
(His will be done.)

Before my Master even adopted me, He knew me. He knew the *leash* (which is the Law) was too harsh for me. Subsequently, He set up a plan that would purchase the *harness* (Grace), on which the leash is attached. This He did to allow me to escape the consequences of my foolishness (Spiritual Death). Every now and then a *cat[1]* crosses my path as my Master walks me through HIS neighborhood. He then reminds me, "Know ye that I am GOD. Ye are the sheep of MY pasture. Psalms 100:3 This is the way, walk ye in it." Psalms 119:1

There will be no greater joy than when I return home and hear my Master declare, "Well done my good and faithful servant. Matt 25:21 Enter, ye, into My gates." Psalms 100:4 I pray that I be not found sleeping as *burglars* try to break in MY Master's fortress. He too, has set an alarm system and has commanded me:

> *Watch, for you know neither the day nor the hour*
> *when I will return.* Matt 25:13

---

[1] Those annoyances that creep into our lives that distract and disrupt our peace.

All men are dogs!

Think about it: most of the time we look at a dog's markings to determine its breed or mixture thereof. Different dogs have different snouts. Likewise, we check their eyes and ears to figure out their breed. After my newfound love of dogs, and with a Godly sense of humor, I examined the offered expression deeper and found the correlation hilarious. Read this story, think about a few of your friends, and see if you agree. All men ARE dogs!

Two thoughts are needed, before you start:
1. The markings I am speaking of are marks of character, not physical traits. When I speak of his eyes, I refer to his I(s) or his self-concept, his ears refer to how alert he is to his Master's call, his nose describes what he seeks or his ability to sniff out troubles. Get it? What he knows. His size talks about the depth of his character!
2. God is his Master; we (women) can only hope to be *Man's Best Friend*!

There are many breeds of *dogs*. You have the sporting group, the hounds, the working group, the terriers, the toys, and I am sure there are more. Of course, many *dogs* are mixed breeds, where the attributes of different breeds have crossed during breeding.

Often, *dogs* are purposely mix-bred to overshadow a negative trait. For example, we have the Rottweiler-Shepherd. The Rott is a heavier, thicker dog. Many people prefer its distinctive color markings. Yet they are more likely to have lethargic *eyes* and are less predictable around children. Moreover, its punched-in looking snout makes it look meaner as its jowls flap, even when it is not growling. When cross-bred, with a German Shepherd, most of the dogs will have the Rott's markings and *thickness* but the

German Shepherd's temperament. The *snout* on the Rott-shep mix is usually longer, and their *eyes* are more inquisitive, giving them a softer more personable facial appearance. They both have a guarding temperament, so their *ears* are both keen. Remember, for now, we are concentrating on their *eyes*, *nose*, *ears* and *size*. So, if you prefer the *thickness* in the Rott, you may want to think about the Rott-Shep mix. The softer *eyes*, longer *snout*, and easier disposition make for a better companion. The pure Rott may be a great *junk yard dog*; but can be a bit mean, and unpredictable, when talking about protecting a family.

I wonder if that is where the expression came from: "It's as plain as the nose on his face."

There is, what I call, the cross over breeds like poodles. Poodles were originally bred as working dogs. They used to hunt. Now, they are chiefly used as *show* dogs. They take diligent grooming with little reward except for the *show*. They are a *dramatic dog* with a very distinctive look, I must say. You can see its breeding a mile away.

I cannot imagine anything worse than thinking you are getting a Doberman, only to find out there is Poodle *in the mix*. That is why I say, "Check the *nose*, *eyes*, AND the *ears*!" The ears will giv'em away every time!

The *sporting group* ranges in *size*. They range from Spaniels, which are usually *medium*, to Pointers and Setters, which can be quite *large*. They are generally good around children, quite energetic, and they usually have a keen *sense of smell*. Sometimes, if not trained well, their playfulness is their undoing.

How many of us have known a *Cocker Spaniel* that is so "happy" he literally bounces off the walls? I must admit, Spaniels are endearing. They are very loyal and really try hard to please. The only problem is that most of the

Spaniels I know lack focus. They are very energetic and seem to have a lot going, but in actuality, they bounce so quickly from one thought to the next that they get almost nothing done.

Pointers, on the other hand, are extremely focused. They will stand and point at the target as long as it takes to *get their point across*. They don't solve a thing; but boy, they WILL point! Do I need to talk about *Setters*? They seem to get *set* on a subject and will not let it go. They will talk circles, but you can bet on it— they will return to the *point* they were originally *set* on.

What about the hounds? There are many types of them: there is the Greyhound, quick on its feet; the Basset Hound, all bark no bite; Beagles, always eager to help—and several more. In general, hounds usually have short hair and do not shed much; that means they are *low maintenance.*

The Bloodhound is known for his nose. When I think of the *Bloodhound*, I picture that "wrinkled old hound" on the old TV show called *The Beverly Hillbillies*, "true blue"(loyal), and not anxious about troubles. When everybody else is running around, he is lying there seemingly without a care. When they finally call on him for help, he gets up and tracks the problem, handles it, and then goes back to his *porch.* Many step over the *old hound dog* thinking him lazy; they just don't realize, he's not lazy–he's confident!

We ladies know a *Hound Dog* when we see one sniffin' around— at nothin' like a hound *dog!*

In my younger years, I thought *Terriers* and *Toys* were the most useless of *dogs.* I used to think of them as always underfoot and nipping at your ankles. However, for the *dog* lover that cannot deal with the larger breeds and the issues their *size* can bring, I see now that the companionship a smaller *dog* brings can mean a lot; little dogs are better at some things.

They are friskier and a bit more energetic. Terriers usually range from *small* to *medium*, while *Toys* are always *small*.

Recently, I learned that Terriers are actually frisky working dogs. They were first bred to hunt rodents and go down into their underground burrows. No wonder *Terriers* are good for chasing the small *pests* that eat away at life's pleasures; that's their breeding.

*Toy*s, on the other hand (and we all know a few), are there to comfort and cheer. They are not much good for anything else, but they do make one feel needed and appreciated— just what the doctor may order sometimes.

They often feel that the whole world is bigger than they are but can be reassured with *toys* and *treats* that are made just for them.

The *working group* is my personal favorite. Oh, are we talking about dogs or *dogs*? They have many different abilities ranging from guard dogs to sled dogs. Some, like huskies, work better in the *cold* difficult times because of their *thick fur*. The *eyes, nose, and ears* are extremely important in the working dog, mainly because there isn't much training you can do with their natures. They tend to be dug into *what comes natural* to them. It often takes sickness or great loss for the *working dog* to change his ways.

How they were treated as a *puppy* has a great deal to do with their adult temperament. If taught well as a puppy, with strict tender love, the full-grown *working dog* is a wonder to behold. When seeking this kind of *dog*, make sure to study their nature very carefully. They HAVE been known to turn on their *Masters*.

Most men want to be classed as Big *Dogs*; I think it is an ego thing. But honestly, there are good traits in all the breeds, and big dogs do have their flaws. Big dogs need room. Their *size* is something that must be considered; they do not do well in *cramped quarters*. They can sometimes play rough, and their *toys* are a bit on the expensive side. Of course, their *toys* cost more; they are made for a *Big Dog*!

Big Dogs equally have big appetites; AND along with a big appetite, comes—big *poop*; it is his nature, he can't change it!

> Note: Many people don't realize that a dog can be trained to use one specific area of the yard for its elimination needs. This is especially helpful when the family enters the *backyard* (the *Big Dog's* turf).
>
> With a well-trained *Big Dog,* you know where NOT to step! And, if you CHOSE to step in his *potty area* you know to *walk carefully* or expect to get *poop* on your *shoes*.

Whatever the case, if you want a *dog*, remember to consider his eyes[2], ears[3], nose[4], and size[5]. And equally, not to be forgotten, his *poop factor*.[6]

Oh, by the way you probably wonder what I think of women— In general, I think they're catty but that's a whole 'nother story.

---

[2] His I's - how self-aware he is.

[3] His listening and alertness to God's call.

[4] His KNOWledge base or source of truth.

[5] The depth of his character!

[6] Must the world watch where they step because HE *commands* the *whole backyard.*

I come to the garden....
Alone?

John 15:4

1991

For the last few years, working in my gardens was a form of quiet time to get aside by myself. This is where the Lord expounded some of His principles. Mind you, my goal was not to feed my family on the harvest of my crop, my deepest joy was caring for my plants, reproducing them, and hearing the Lord rustle in the breeze.

When I first started gardening, there was a dear friend that shared the *"principle of the seed"* with me. She told me that most plants have a seed, somewhere within, just for the picking; you just need to know what you are looking for. My garden became a little experiment lab. I started with the easy seeds like watermelon, green peppers, cucumbers, and hot peppers. I took seeds from the food I had in the refrigerator, dried them, planted them, and watched them grow. I soon moved to the more mysterious seeds like marigolds and kale. In those cases, I bought a package of seeds, grew the plant, and watched to see where the seed reproduced itself. In ten years, I have yet to buy those seeds again. Each year in the fall, I let the plants *go to seed*. That is when I leave them growing well past their normal harvesting time until they produce seeds. After that, I harvest the seeds and plant them the following spring. Even when I moved, I just planted the seeds in the new location.

Now, almost all the flowers and vegetables, in my gardens, are growing from seeds harvested from previous years. Every now and then I add new seeds to learn or discover a new concept in the growing process. Last year, I had my greatest triumph. I grew cannas (pronounced CAN-a) from seeds. I originally planted roots, grew the plants, harvested their seeds, and then, successfully grew cannas from seeds.

For those that do not know what cannas are, a canna is a tall decorative flower that grows to about three feet tall. Their large green leaves are the first things that show as they come from the ground. When it reaches almost three feet, the flower starts to develop. I have seen yellow, red, and, I think, orange cannas. Like other lilies, they usually grow in patches as they spread each year by sprouting new growth from the roots.

A friend gave me some canna root (sometimes called bulbs) from her yard; they were quite big and looked like small, sweet potatoes with several bulb-like knots.

It took a while, but I finally learned to plant the bulbs with the sprouts pointing up. Then after a couple of good years, I let the cannas *go to seed*. They produced black seeds that looked a lot like black BB gun pellets. Next, it crossed my mind to try growing some canna from the seeds; so, when I was gathering my marigold seeds, I gathered seeds from the cannas too. I threw them into a flowerpot, with some soil, and waited anxiously to see them sprout. I waited and waited and waited. Several weeks passed; I got impatient and stirred the soil. The seeds had neither split nor cracked. Okay—I waited and waited some more. Then, like a little kid, I stirred the soil again. They STILL hadn't changed. This was, now, a matter of months. I gave up and decided that maybe the seed needed some special treatment. I decided to stick to using the roots. I stuck the flowerpot, with the seeds and soil, into a corner; planning to use the soil when needed. I went on with the rest of the garden. Months later, as I was cleaning the yard, I noticed the flowerpot. There they were—several canna leaves sprouting. What a thrill! By leaving them alone, they grew!

Truly a case of - *Let go; let God!*

There were object lessons around every turn.

As you can probably see, the main purpose, of the gardens, was discovery. While learning about the seeds, I enjoyed learning about the nature of the plants too.

- The tomato—its roots nourished but did not support the weight of the plant when it was bearing fruit. As a result, it needed some type of support as the tomatoes grew.

- While most of my vegetables (like kale, cucumbers, and squash) grew just fine in the *regular* garden, the green peppers grew much better in the big pots along the side of the garden.

- The string beans were genuinely interesting. Watching them grow was another thrill. First the vine grew. Afterwards, tiny little blossoms bloomed. Then, bean pods started to form. I wasn't sure how long to leave the pods on the vine; but I finally found a happy median. They grew best when you did not let the vines twist among themselves and plucked the pods weekly. Then, the vine would produce pod after pod. In the fall, I let the string beans stay on the vine until the pod turned brown and cracked open. Then I harvested seeds for the next year's planting.

- Several types of vines grew around the fence of my vegetable garden. I recognized one of them as honeysuckle because of its flowers' sweet fragrance when it bloomed.

One morning, I was weaving a tender vine growth into the fence, and the thought *Train up a child in the way he should go* popped into my head. I stopped and contemplated, *Lord you certainly do have a sense of humor.* I thought about the lessons I had learned and realized the garden was a microcosm of a well-orchestrated community.

- The *general population* worked well in proximity. They could overcome the everyday hardships of *firm soil* and *rockiness*, their roots were firm and the heat, of life's trials (direct sunlight), did not make them wither. Though sometimes sparse, the *soil's general nutrients* were enough to supply their needs. Their individual natures accentuated each other, and they were strong enough to thrive in the *garden* as long as the *rain* (blessings) fell regularly, and *weeds* (sins) were pulled quickly.

- The *weaker population* needed to be accommodated with more careful nurturing. They needed the soil to be *treated* with drainage, nutrients, and packing of the soil. The condition of the soil needed to be controlled. This was not a bad thing, at all. They just needed a little more *Tender Lovin' Care.* Soon, with the specialized care of the *Gardener,* they, too, would be transplanted back into the garden and be productive members of the community.

- Some bore *heavy* fruit and needed to be supported. This brought to mind members of the community that carry *heavy* responsibilities. They blossomed within their supporting structures so that their fruit could grow to its greatest potential.

    I thought of the single parent, the struggling student, the family burnt out by fire, the farmer in a time of drought—all those trying to succeed but needing that initial help. Their *fruits* are sometimes hard to bear. They are burdened with the weight of the worries of the community, but a network of support is there to enable them to stand the ballast. If not, their *fruit* would *lay on the ground* where life's *worms* would get to it.

Each society needs a *policing agency* to "Guard the *Perimeter*".

- ‣ The marigold*s*, by their mere presence, warded off intruders. They stood in their bright array with such a permeating fragrance that *beast* and *bugs* alike would not dare cross their ranks.

The string bean vine (the garden's religious *sub-community*), if left on its own, would strangle itself in an ever-twisting array of details. The Master *Gardener* must keep the vines on course— each vine carrying out its specified *ministry* to the blooms and pods that it nourishes.

- ‣ *String beans* gathered at harvest, for food, are generally gathered while they are *tender and sweet.*[7] They share their *nutrients*[8] as part of the total *meal,*[9] along with the *protein,*[10] various *grains,*[11] other *vegetables,*[12] and the *dessert plate.*[13] All of which should be nourishing and appealing to the *tastebuds.*[14] Later, the beans that were chosen for replanting are *buried*[15] and spring forth new plants[16]—as part of a new harvest.

The honeysuckle and other *clinging vines* were admirable. They provided shade for some areas of the garden as they beautified the fence line. When they blossomed, they provided a sweet aroma that was smelt yards away. Though quite lovely,

---

[7] Humble and kind
[8] Gifts from God
[9] General Church Outreach
[10] Pastor/Teacher
[11] Faith, Healing, Discernment
[12] Service, Craftsmanship, Helps
[13] Hospitality
[14] To reach others for Christ
[15] Death of self
[16] Discipleship

---

the vines could prove detrimental to the garden if not trained to dress the fence line instead of growing amongst the plants.

> Like children, the clinging vines had to be trained or they would overrun the *garden*. While most of the year the vines were green and leafy (easily seen/ evident to the eye), there were moments that each vine "came into season". The honeysuckle vine, as our continued example, just *dresses the fence line* with the other vines. However, when it *flowers*, the fragrance of honeysuckle permeates the neighborhood.

> Just like these clinging vines, our children *dress* our community. They stand around the border of life watching and learning. As evident in today's society, if children are not trained, they too will begin to overrun the community. They can even go as far as choking the life out of it. But if *trimmed and trained* in their youth, they *come into season* when we see them blossom and emit their *fragrance* or bring forth their *fruit*.

I honestly believe that one of my greatest heavenly joys will be tending the garden around my mansion. I cannot wait!

Imagine—

The ceaseless ages of lessons to learn from my big brother,

the MASTER Gardener.

Learning My Lessons Come First

1992

When my sons were preschool aged, they loved to watch a video, of an old 1976 TV musical named Pinocchio starring Danny Kaye and Sandy Duncan. They loved singing one of its little songs. The main line was "I've learned my lesson, and the lesson I've learned is learning my lessons come first!" As preschoolers, they thought repeating the tongue twister and understanding its logic was the coolest thing since sliced bread. They spent hours (even days) singing it. Many years later, when my nephew, Brighton, came to spend a weekend, the song came to mind, and I used its influence to teach some principles.

> *That weekend, I overheard them calling me Drill Sergeant—behind my back, of course. They thought they were insulting me; I took it as a compliment! Many a good man has been developed through the training of a diligent drill sergeant.*

I "invited" Brighton to spend a weekend with us because of his misbehavior at school. I thought he needed to *learn a few lessons.* Since spending early mornings working in my garden always opened my eyes to the principles of God, I could not imagine any better source of object lessons.

That first night, our plan was to wake up early in the morning and head out to work in the yard. Instead, because of Brighton's procrastination, we did not start to work until 8:00 a.m., which I knew would catch us later. I kept that lesson *in my pocket* for the near future.

When we finally got ready to work in the garden, my nephew learned his first *lesson* when the thought of bugs kept him from wanting to work.

Lesson: Don't let the *bugs* get you down.
That is what *gloves* are for!

Principles: Don't sweat the little things.
Do not let the annoyances of life keep you from achieving your goals. Find a way!

His first job was to pull weeds in the garden. That was the easiest *lesson* of all.

Lesson: Young weeds are easier to pull before growing a strong root.

Principle: It is easier to handle problems and bad habits when they are new before they get *established*.

The garden is in the far-right corner of the backyard with the evergreens forming a fence line upward towards the house. With the garden in that section of the yard, it is nice to work in the early morning hours. If you start between 6:30 a.m. and 7:00 a.m., the air is fresh, the streets are quiet, and the house behind ours serves to shade you for a while.

We finished pulling the weeds and the next job was to trim the trees. The trees were growing close to each other and, when trimmed, they looked more like a ten-foot hedge than a group of trees. But, at this point they were wildly unshaped and

overhung the sidewalk.

As we stood at the end of the line of trees with hedge trimmers in hand, I asked Brighton what he thought they would look like when we finished. He replied just as I thought he would, "Straight and tall."

We pulled and tied limbs back. We trimmed and whacked. Finally, after an hour or so, we were finished. We went back to that same spot at the end of the row of trees, and I asked him what he saw. He was surprised! They were not straight at all; instead, they were curvy. We trimmed them back, therefore allowing people to easily pass on the sidewalk. But instead of forcing them into an unnatural *squared-off* shaping, they were allowed to keep their natural curves. "Okay", I said, "what is the lesson?" He smiled a big grin.

Lesson: Not all hedges trim straight and tall. They can show their natural beauty when kept within the limits.

Principle: You can develop your individualism;
             but, stay within the limits.

We had finished our work in the garden and slowly, as the sun began to cross the sky, we noticed its warm heat penetrating our muscles and heating our joints. Just as we finished the trees and started cleaning the cuttings, the sun came around the corner and was no longer blocked by the house behind mine. We were definitely ready for a drink of cool water. I asked my nephew for the key to the house. He started to point slowly and said, "I laid it over therrre…"

Suddenly, he noticed the key was missing. He pointed to an area on the ground where we had gone back and forth several times with trees and branches while cleaning up cuttings.

Looking for the key, we went up and down, back and forth, and then up and down again. I wanted him to feel the pressure of the lost key. After several long minutes of searching, I pulled out the key from my pocket. Earlier, I had noticed him when he put it on the ground and took it when he was not looking.

Lesson: It is easier to find a key in a pocket.
Principle: Take a minute to put things in their place. It saves time and worry in the long run.

We went it the house and got our water, then continued our work. We had one more job to do on the curbside of the trees before we moved to the shady, inside area of the yard. We still had to wash and wax the car. The sun was warm and the cool water from the hose was a relief against the building heat.

> *Note:* The time was about 10:00 a.m. The car takes almost exactly an hour to wash and wax. The sun sizzles at 11:00 a.m. Do the math!

At just about 10:45, while waxing, the sun was HOT! Then, I pulled that procrastination lesson out my pocket.

Lesson: Finish your work before the sun comes around the corner.
Principle: Do it now... It only gets harder later.
Brighton's Interpretation:
Make the best of your life before it's too late.

At about 11:00 a.m., as we were finishing the car, we talked about the process. Brighton wanted to skip cleaning the inside of the car because the heat was just about unbearable.

Lesson: The car isn't clean unless it's clean inside and out.
Principle: Your outside (what you show to the world) may be clean, but you are not clean unless your inside is clean too. God sees through our *tinted windows*.

Waxing the car taught another lesson.

Lesson: Wipe ALL the wax off, or it WILL show up later.
Principle: Surely your sins WILL find you out.

After finishing the car, I thought we were ready for a break. Brighton thought this was a good time to play with Nikki, our dog, and started trying to get her to chase a ball around the yard. She was lying in the cool shade of the trees and simply looked at him with a look that meant, *boy, do you know how hot it is?*

Lesson: Even a dog will not leave the shade to play in the heat.
Principle: Use the good sense God has given you.
Brighton's Interpretation:
             That is just plain out *unnecessary roughness.*

Since he still had plenty of energy, we continued to work. To keep from overheating, we worked in the shaded yard and were ready for another job using water. What better job than washing the dog? She loved it because the water felt great.

This next lesson was fun AND funny! Nikki was being especially patient because the cool water felt so very good. Brighton scrubbed and tugged as she stood patiently allowing his clumsy escapade.

He lathered her from head to tail and, as he finished brushing her tail, he took the hose to rinse her. I was standing in front of her holding her leash and took two steps backward— and smiled. Brighton standing at her side, saw my smile, but kept on going. He didn't think to ask what I was smiling about.

Lesson: When wetting a dog, stand in front of it;
             OR— expect to get wet when they shake.
Principle: Anticipate!

The rest of the day was rather easy going.
Lessons were constantly close at hand:

Lesson: Get the big pieces, then sweep the dust.
Principle: Do the obvious; then, do the details.

Lesson: Dirt hides. Find it!
Principle: Don't just do the obvious. Search!
Do the job (whatever it is) thoroughly.

Lesson: Leaving leftovers on the porch will attract ants.
Principle: Bad habits attract trouble.

Lesson: He who wears baggy pants should always wear a belt.
Principle: Some embarrassments are self-inflicted.

The final lesson for the day was:
Lesson: If momma ain't happy, ain't nobody happy!
Principle: Honor your MOTHER and Father, in the Lord,
that YOUR days may be long on THIS earth!
Exod. 20:12

2009 recap

Looking back at these lessons, I think I learned more that weekend than my nephew. God gave me a review of many life lessons while spending time, with Brighton, *right in my own backyard.* For him, I was just planting seeds; for me, God was repotting full grown plants into richer soil.

The Bible says to train your children as you come and go in your daily lives that YOURS, and your child's, days may be multiplied. Deut. 11:19 , 21

Lesson: God uses our children to train US for His kingdom.

Like a Needle to the Pole

Is keeping the Commandments a form of legalism? "We're saved by Grace!" is the usual cry of the righteous. But, when someone does some socially unethical act, the Ten Commandments are pulled out, and dusted off, to show the poor wayward soul the measure of their unrighteousness.

There cannot be a standard for some and anarchy for others. The same *ruler* measures us all. The Ten Commandments, being the written image of God's character, are the living measurement of His righteousness. As the Bible says, if not for the Law, we would not know sin. _{Rom. 3:20}

It is easy to expect our youth to endure *as needles to the pole*; they have not lived long enough to develop their own system. What about adults; are we excused by Grace?

The Bible says, "God forbid." _{Rom. 6:15}

Well then! Think a minute; if we are the needles and the Commandments are the pole, why do we have such problems? We should be able to line up to the pole by mere proximity, right?

No, the one unmentioned agent is He that is actively aligning the needle. Needles only respond to a magnetized pole. So, though we say *as a needle to the pole*, the needle is in truth responding to the unseen magnetic force. The pole, consequently, only serves as a visual manifestation of the unseen working of the magnetic force. I therefore conclude that keeping the Commandments become a form of gravitated pull. As the Spirit draws, we align ourselves to the character of God.

If it was up to the needle to align to the pole, with nothing from which to draw but its own power, THAT would be legalism.

However in contrast, the magnetic drawing of the needle to the pole is the working of Grace Himself.

In view of that, the complete all-encompassing answer is:

Yes, we ARE saved by* grace!

We, like needles, are drawn by Grace's magnetic wooing to the pole of His uprightness.

*The word *by* in this case is a verb of action, meaning: "through the medium of, at the hand of, in the name of, or because of".

Amazing Grace!
How sweet the sound,
That saved a wretch like me!
I once was lost, but now I'm found.
Was blind, but now I see.

If You Can't Stand the Heat, Get Out of the Kitchen!

(or maybe you just need some water)

1993

Within me there is a controversy about the Marthas of the world. The Bible says that Mary chose the good thing.[17] Does that mean that Martha should not have been in the kitchen? But that gives way to the question, "What happens if all the Martha's sit down?"

Was the problem that Martha was in the kitchen or was the problem that Martha was NOT at the *feet of Christ*? I propose that Martha should have been both. We (the Marthas) have been blessed with a divine gift, the ability to *stir* and *dwell*. Our main problem is usually that we get so busy *stirring* that we forget that we are simultaneously supposed to be *dwelling*. Our minds drift off focus, and we start looking around the *kitchen*.

Another problem we have is that the Marys in our lives have come to EXPECT *dinner* to be ready. They do not realize the stress that causes a Martha. See, we are here to serve, and serve we must. At least that is what we think when we get off focus.

It is easy for us to get so caught up in WHAT we are serving and forget WHO we are serving. Like my sons say, "We're *caught up in the 'Kool-Aide' and don't even know the flavor.*"

It is also natural for us to give until we are empty.

---

[17] Luke 10:38-42

We have to stop feeling guilty when *Marys* have to wait a little while before *dinner* is ready. I believe Christ will ring the *dinner bell* only AFTER He has spent time in the kitchen with Martha.

I venture to say that if Martha had held her piece, Christ may have gone into the kitchen, Himself, and helped her. If only she had seen the bigger picture. She may not have heard the message He had given the group; but He would have had a story tailor-made for her need.

Think about it, oh ye Marthas, God speaks to our needs SPECIFICALLY when we do not get to hear what He told the crowd. We just have to keep *dwelling*.

If you are a Martha, you probably find yourself often, in the *kitchen*. Don't let that throw you. The *kitchen* is not the problem; check your spiritual proximity to Jesus.

God has a blessing specifically for you. Just keep *dwelling*.

Now, a word to you Marys out there:
> Have compassion for the Marthas in your life.
> Remember, Marthas are people too.

Yes, Marthas may seem tired when you have plenty of energy.
> They work hard to make others more comfortable.

Yes, Martha-s may seem too busy.
> They are usually doing two or three jobs at once.
> > Martha-s are like that.

Yes, Martha-s may seem anti-social.
> Many Marthas tend to move in small groups.
> > Often, just the *kitchen* staff.

But Marthas do love people.
> Otherwise, they would not love the *serving line*.

Do you want to BEFRIEND a Martha?
> There is usually no better way than to bring your
> Martha a cup of *water*[18] when the *kitchen* is hot.

---

[18] John 4:13-14

Walk Softly and
Carry a Big Stick

Why Not Just Catch the Bus?

1994

Lately, Timothy (my eldest son) has been saying that the hard times he has been experiencing have served as "Life Lessons". True, he has been learning, and faced each new experience with the enthusiasm that depicts his age. A matter of fact, this is the same son who led the repeated childhood ditty "The lesson I learned is learning my lesson comes first." Then, why should I expect him to approach life, as a young man, any differently? Why have I had this uneasy feeling that I just cannot explain?

Anyone frequently driving down a particular road near my home has become acutely aware of an unusual little man who stands by one of the stoplights with a BIG walking stick, much in the fashion of Moses holding his rod towards the Red Sea[19].

> Actually, the Bible says Moses stretched out his hand. I probably saw him holding a rod in the movies.

Much like that, this man raises his *rod* towards the traffic light and has come to the delusional conclusion that HE controls the light, and by reason, HE controls the traffic.

---

[19] Exodus 14:21

When you think of him only with a surface thought, it IS rather funny to see the old man waving this great big stick at the light. I have never seen him bother anyone. I have never even seen him speak to anyone. He simply *controls* his light.

Then again, when you bear in mind that this is some mother's son, it is a bit sad. It seems like *his light* could be the only thing he can control in a life that may be like a runaway train. Thus, he finds safety there. It is him and his stick against the light, and he has won! Each time that light changes *on his command* is a victory for him.

Somewhere along the line, this poor soul has lost sight of the fact that the light will change with or without him. The light WILL change. So, faithfully day and night, people can ride up and down this road and see him *on post*. He has lived the rhythm of the signal so long that he raises his rod right at the split second before the light changes. He seems convinced it is he who allows drivers to continue down the road.

I thought of this man the other day when my son said he was learning yet another of life's lessons. That is when I realized why I was so very unsettled. Somehow my son has gotten off track and has been trying to learn to *control the light*. But the light WILL change! We cannot control it. We can get in its rhythm and raise our *rods,* but the light WILL change with or without our help.

> Yes, we try to avoid the *stoplights* of life. We speed up a little when the *light* is yellow. We slow down a little when we see in the distance that the *light* is red. We try to avoid stopping as much as possible, but each of us hit a *RED light* every now and then.

The lesson is not in controlling the light.
The light WILL change!
The REAL lesson is in how we *continue down the road,*
when the light changes. Selah!

I prayed, "Wow, Lord thank you! I prayed for a story that ended this part of my life's diary on a high note. You answer even the smallest of hearts desires!"

"But God, you gave me the title to this story BEFORE I wrote it. The title you gave mentioned a bus.
The story seems complete, but what about the bus?"

God answered,

I am the bus. Let me take you from destination to destination and you will not even have to worry about the rhythm of the lights.
Rest in me.
Abide in me.
I'll take you there~

I told you.

God is truly *awesome!*

A Journey Continued

Have you ever driven down a long highway and suddenly realize that you do not remember the last several miles you just travelled? All of a sudden, something shakes your attention! You check your bearings and see you are still on the correct road, but for whatever reason you have lost track of the miles as they passed. Sometimes all we can do is hit "fast-forward", catch-up to where we are, and start from there.

My sons are grown now and gone out on their own. I cannot believe it! It was only yesterday when it seemed the teenage years would never end. Now I look back over my shoulder and see the things I wish I had done. Things I never had time to do. Things that I thought were insignificant I see, with 20/20 hindsight, as eminently significant.

When God gave me the first set of stories, I was not sure what to do with them. I KNEW the last one was the last one; I did not realize it was the last of a group. I have spent the last few years happily marinating in the lessons God poured into my spirit. Suddenly, He called me back to writing when I heard Him knocking—

I Stand at the Door and Knock

1999

It never fails to amaze me how God, in his infinite greatness, continues to speak to me in such simple ways. I recently asked the Lord on several occasions to make me a living witness. As usual, He has answered that prayer with a growth experience.

I have a young neighbor who accompanies me to church most weekends. I go to the early morning worship service and then return to our neighborhood to get him and his younger brothers. Together, we return to attend Bible study and mid-morning worship. We have been doing this for several months. We started in the fall, continued through winter, limped through spring, and now, we are waning as summer begins.

In the fall, as the leaves changed colors, the world was in preparation for change and a mindset acceptant of new experiences was predictable. Something new and different seemed quite the adventure. Going to church was a new experience full of the unknown and new expectations—just the thing little boys find appealing.

During the winter months, the church was a warm, cozy place to be. There was a confident expectation of joy in the experience. Plans and commitments were made with the anticipation of summer fun. Keeping an edge of excitement and anticipation of what might happen when the weather was better, no one wanted to miss a weekend. The thought of each coming weekend seemed far from the next.

As spring arrived, it brought rainy-day sleep-in mornings, the smell of fresh air, and the sprouting of new life. With the fading away of the gloom of winter, spring brought with it the hope for summer fun and marked the air with a new awakening. The main thought being, "If I just hold on, summer will be here soon."

Now, summer IS here. School IS out. Free time has come! But the plans that seemed like so much fun, when dreamed about in the winter, seem more like drudgery and hard work in the heat of the summer sun. A fast pace of activities seems to crowd us in the summer, leaving little time for the winter plans that were so anticipated.

Isn't that the way it is though? Just as we have things all planned and in order, things creep up in our lives calling for our attention. Sometimes we are choosing between pleasing ourselves and pleasing God. Other times we find ourselves with emergencies that we feel we have to handle for safety's sake. Whether it is a broken toy, a broken heart, or a broken window, either can take several hours away from our plans. When we look up, the sunny day has passed, and none of the intended plans came to fruition.

During this past month or so, I have found myself returning home after the morning service and knocking on my young neighbor's front door to no avail. They do not have a phone and the bell does not work; for that reason, I knock. I am there each week knocking because each week they say they want to go. In their hearts, they want to go, but, for whatever reason, when it is time to get up and answer the door. They just don't FEEL like it.

Today, as I stand here knocking, I find myself listening to see if ANYONE in the house is awake. Maybe someone else can answer the door and THEY can wake my friend. Occasionally, I wait for traffic to finish passing before I knock, thinking the noise of passing trucks and buses may be so loud that my knock will not be heard. I did this several times before I was conscious of the irony.

How often is God knocking [20] only to find that I have rolled over to ignore His call? [21] Each week I say, "Yes, Lord. I want to go." [22] But, when it's time to get up, I roll over.

In life's fall seasons, I look forward to changing all those old habits that have held me back. [23] In the winter moments, I make plans with much excitement and the best of intentions. Spring moments come with rainy-day sleep-in mornings [24] and my plans melt into a haze of busyness in the heat of the summer blaze. [25]

How many *trucks* does God have to wait to pass? Where is my *heart-house* located? Is it right along the highway, or is it on a country back road? Am I listening for the quiet knock? Why not fix the doorbell? Why am I not dressed and sitting on the front porch? Do I truthfully want to go?

Lord, help my un-readiness. [26]
The things I want to do, I do not.
The things I wish not to do; they I do. [27]
Only you are able to wake me to answer the door! [28]

--Selah

---

[20] Revelation 3:20
[21] Matthew 26:41
[22] Isaiah 6:8
[23] Philippians 3:13-14
[24] Mark 13:35 - 36
[25] Matt 13:6
[26] Mark 9:23 - 24
[27] Galatians 5:17; Romans 7:15
[28] Ephesians 3:20; Philippians 4:13; Jude 24-25

In Knowledge and Ammunition

2000

Have you ever listened carefully to a young child recite a song, poem, phrase, or scripture? Sometimes they are simply hilarious. They tend to substitute words that are familiar for the words that are beyond their comprehension, like the following:

<u>Who brought</u> stripes and bright stars
<u>to the pair of us fight?</u> "
Or ... He maketh me lie down <u>with</u> green <u>pastors.</u>

*One may want to make note of the phraseology the young mind has chosen. There can sometimes be much insight hidden in their restructured thought. The songwriter probably had great meaning in the phrase "Heaven's **table land"**. Though I caught it years ago, even now, I find more comfort in Heaven's **stable** land.*

Several years in a row, my allergies were so terrible that I lost my voice for weeks at a time. At church, I was miserable when I could not participate during song service.

Years earlier, I attended sign language classes when my sons earned badges in their Pathfinders' Club, so the thought of signing instead of singing was not as foreign as it may have been to some people. I asked a good friend to teach me a few more words to help me fill in the gaps. Then I had a fairly good vocabulary and could again *sing* praises.

When using sign language, you sign the MEANING rather than the actual words themselves. For example, in Dottie Rambo's song "We Shall Behold Him," for "The stars shall applaud Him with thunders of praise," I signed, "The stars shall applaud him like thunder praise." And for "The sweet light, in His eyes, shall enhance those a-waiting" I signed, "The light, in His eyes, shall change those that are here."

Internally translating the meaning of what is being said (or sung) has a way of deeply enhancing the worship experience. You no longer just sing the words that you have known a lifetime. You have to hear them, translate in your head, glean their message, find words you know how to sign and repeat that message, and do it all before the congregation moves on to the next line. It makes you do a mental dance that drives the worship from your soul to your fingertips. Your brain is so involved that there is not time for distracting thoughts. For me, it was a profound experience of the mountaintop caliber.

It was then I first learned how it felt to totally praise and worship with my whole heart. Each year, when my voice returned, I habitually slipped back into the old habit of singing the words by memory. This year, for the very first time, I learned to have true worship while still having my voice.

I believe the fact that I so often just sang the words to a song, without listening to myself, was why it took so long for me to hear what I was in fact saying. I had been repeating the good old *gospel catch phrases* without even thinking about their meanings.

I have said the featured phrase countless times without any thought. The other day it crossed my mind and I realized that, in fact, I was shooting bullets of knowledge at people, and I almost *laughed out loud.*

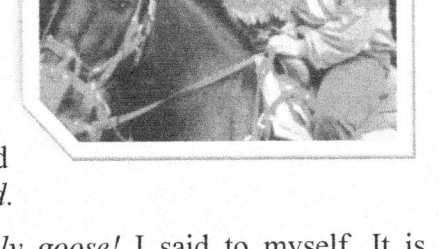

It's ADMONITION, you silly goose! I said to myself. It is, "Bring them in knowledge and ADMONITION of the Lord"[29] not –Bring 'em in knowledge and AMMUNITION of the Lord.

---

[29] I Corinthians 10:11

Super-Fishial Love

April

It is weird how my new hobby crept up on me. I didn't realize it until I found myself saying to an attendant in the aquarium store, "This stuff sounds like raising kids. I just sent my last child off to boot camp. Now I'm starting all over again with fish."

Yes, I am officially an aquariumnist; and have been for a while. The moment the words crossed my lips, I realized that I had unintentionally avoided the empty nest syndrome by filling my nest with fish.

I am now maintaining two aquariums; in fact, three but the third is only five gallons, so I am not counting it. My main tank is a seventy-two-gallon bow-front Discus tank. The second tank is a thirty-gallon Goldfish tank.

The Discus tank is a community tank. Which is essentially an oxymoron because a community tank is usually a variety of fish species living together, supporting each other equally. Describing the community tank by one of its inhabitants (in this case the discus) says that the "community" is in effect a *disc-ocracy*.

> Theocracy means governed by God. Hierocracy means governed by clergy; and monocracy means dictatorship. Then, DISC-ocracy would mean governed by discus, which is unmistakably an appropriate description of this tank.

I started my tank with two Discus fish, an Angel fish, and a couple of bottom feeders. They were beautiful but I found them quite boring to watch. The Discus, though very elegant, do not do anything. The Angel was much the same. Unless you enjoy watching live vacuum cleaners, the bottom feeders were not fun to watch either. I added other species to add some "spice" to the tank.

Now that I have changed to the community tank concept, the tank consists of four Discus, two Angels, two Elephant Nose Fish, three glass catfish, three armored catfish, six emperor neons, four stick algae eaters, two Siamese algae eaters, and one pleco algae eater; each fish was specially chosen to enhance the development of the overall community.

My Goldfish tank, on the other hand, is much simpler. There are three goldfish thus far: a Lion-Head and two Fantails. Their whole purpose is to eat, swim, and grow.

June

The Discus tank is the topic for discussion this time.

For those that do not know Discus, from the side they appear big and round and when seen head-on they are very thin, much like a similar fish called Silver Dollars. Discus, however, are usually very colorful. Some are shades of orangey-red, some have a turquoise sheen, some simply brown with a specific stripped design. Then of course, there are mixtures of all these traits when the species crossbreed.

I just noticed that, up until now, when typing the names of the various fish there were certain fish I rated above others. The *Show* Fish listed above have their names capitalized, while the supporting fish are listed in lowercase. I don't believe it; I did all of that subconsciously.

Some time has passed since I started this story. I was sure that the story was to speak on the way we unjustly classify the importance of people by the titles they do (or do not) have [30], *but though the thought is legitimate, it doesn't seem to be developing.*

---

[30] Romans 12:4-5

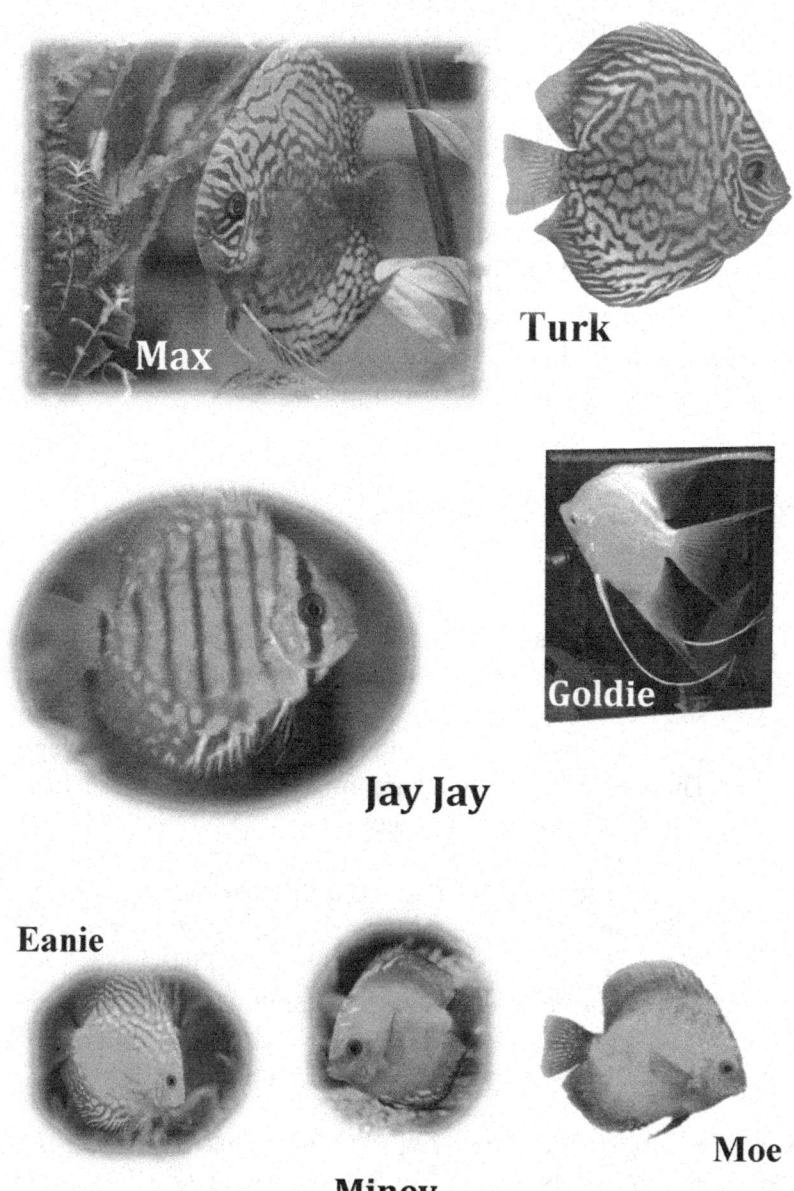

Max

Turk

Jay Jay

Goldie

Eanie

Miney

Moe

These are not pictures of my actual fish, but they are so similar that you get a real idea of their beauty.

July

From the day I brought him home, Max (short for Maximus) took over the tank. A Turquoise and Red crossbred discus, he was always the most beautiful of all the fish in the tank. He decided who could stay and who could not. As a result of controlling their food intake, he decided how big he would allow them to grow. If he didn't want a fish to survive, he would harass them and not allow them to eat.

Max grew from 4" to almost 7" in diameter. He got so bossy in the main tank that it was necessary to remove him to allow the others to grow. I bought a thirty-gal tank and moved Max into another room all to himself, except a few supporter fish. So now, I have four tanks going.

The *show* fish left in the main tank are the following:
Jay-Jay, a Turquoise-faced Heckle discus.
   I bought him less than a month ago. He is about 6".

Turk, a Turquoise-Diamond discus,
   I bought him at about 3" and he has grown to 5".

Moe, (Eanie and Miney died, and there was no Meany).
   I bought three discus at the youngest age, called quarter-sized because of their diameter. Their names came from the fact that I could not decide which one to buy. So, I bought all three. Moe has grown to be about 4".

Goldie, a Yellow-Ghost angelfish, was one of my first fish and has grown from 1½" to about 3" (not including her long trailing fin).

The Supremes and the Pips (not pictured) are a school of Glass catfish. At first, I bought only three. When they started to do a synchronized swimming pattern every time I played music, I dubbed them *the*

Supremes. I enjoyed them so much that I added two more and called the new ones *the Pips*.

In addition, there are supporter fish: a pleco, a stick-fish, and two Siamese Algae Eaters named Cheech & Chong (two silly fish that chase each other endlessly around the tank).

The lesson God was teaching me, through the fish, had nothing to do with the fish at all. The superficial way we place value has always been the lesson. Is something more important ONLY because of its cost or beauty? Is the shinier bauble more valuable? Does something bring more joy; just because it cost more? Is someone more important because of his or her income or title? I was learning that the nature (or character) designs the worth, not its superficial documentations.

September,

Over the years of running these tanks, some of the fish survived and others did not. When the first *supporter* fish died, I counted it a fact of life in keeping a fish tank. However, when the first Discus died, it hit me harder. I thought about the beginning of this story and realized all their death was a fact of life. Some are going to make it and others may not. In a COMMUNITY tank, I should not favor any fish above the other; they all have a purpose in the tank.

I opened this story several times to write about one thing or another I had learned, but each time God has said, "Not yet." The passing thoughts were lessons unto themselves worthy of mentioning, but a deeper expounded story never came.

1) I learned how to keep the pH balanced. If the pH level was too high, it would cause some fish so much stress they could die; pH levels too low could kill others.

   This reminded me about God's loving care. He balances my life and the stressors thereof to keep them within my tolerance level. I Cor. 10:13

2) I learned to keep the live plants in check. If left to grow without grooming, they would crowd the tank and change the pH:

> *Even good things can come to overcrowd our lives, and cause undue stress, if not kept in balance.*
> Mark 4:19

3) I realized that the fish were dependent on my care. There was nothing they could do; except swim, eat, and grow. If I did not make something available, they did not have it:

> *What a good God we serve! Everything we have is only because God has provided it.* Matt 6:31-33

October

I continued to wait for God's leading with this story and more than a few times God said, "Not yet!" but now He says, "It is time". Eccles.3:1 Indeed, the Human *Community Tank* in which I live, is God's greater lesson.

Last week, I went away on a business trip. For several weeks preceding the training, my pastor's teachings were about "finding ministry moments", so this became an opportune time to search for them.

Whenever I stay in hotels, I try to make friendly, purposeful acquaintance with several of the hotel employees, my room attendant being one. In the past, I have participated in nonverbal communication with them. I chose nonverbal because so often they do not speak English, and many times I never in fact speak to the person. I always try to leave a tip each morning before leaving the room and try to recognize them in the hallway as I come and go. Usually, the attendant will say thank you in some way like fancy folded towels, folding down the bed, a sparkle to the room, or sometimes extra soap.

When I left my tips, this time, the room attendant outdid herself. Each day I returned to my room, she did something extra special. The third day was the charm. Noticing that I used the ice bucket each afternoon, she left a thoughtful surprise.

> The only ice machine on each floor was to the right of the elevators. All the rooms were to the left of the elevator. My room was almost the last one and was therefore at the other end of the hallway. Every day on return from class, I went to the room, got the ice bucket, went all the way back down the hall to get ice, and then returned to the room. No big deal, just inconvenient.

That day when I returned to my room for lunch break, there was a bucket of ice waiting for me. When I left the room to return to class, I saw my attendant in another room. I held up my thermos of ice water and said, "Thanks!" She gave me a great big smile.

That evening I remembered the pastor's *ministry moments*. Also, I realized that this attendant spoke English and there would not be a communication barrier. I prayed for guidance.

In the morning, I wrote a note for the attendant telling her not to clean the room. Instead, I wanted her to use that time to read some scriptures. I highlighted and bookmarked these in the hotels Gideon's Bible: Genesis 2:1-3, Exodus 20:1-17, John 3:16, Ephesians 6:10-14, Revelation 22:14, and finally Revelation 22:20-21.

> God gave me His message from Genesis to Revelation, a power walk through the scriptures. I marked some in pink and some in yellow. The note said to read the yellows to meet Jesus. The pinks were for her to review if she already knew Him.

I straightened the room and left the note along with my regular tip, with the marked Bible. However, when I entered the hallway, I noticed that there was a different attendant on duty that day. I thought of returning and removing the note, but I decided to leave it. I prayed for God to bless my offering and went to class. When I returned, my room glowed; it was immaculate. There was a note left that said, *Thanks so much! I needed that. Yes, I know Jesus. My father is a pastor, but I've strayed away. I read all the scriptures.*

I was on cloud nine. The Ministry Moment was successful. This success sweetened the whole trip: are we not *Fishers of Men*?[31]

> For months God has been speaking to me through this story about classifying HIS *fish*. Here in a simple *community tank* in Pennsylvania, God presented an opportunity for me to use what He had been teaching.
>
> One of His *support fish* needed to be fed. Not that I consider myself a *show fish*; but I was able to control a corner in my tank just long enough to allow His *fish* to receive some *food*.

Reminded of my Glass Catfish, *the Supremes*, I too *dance* transparently before the Lord to the rhythm of HIS music— May others see Jesus THROUGH me!

---

[31] Matthew 4:19

Home in-a Dis Kingdom

For months, people in my life "pushed my buttons". At home, work, on the bus, everywhere! I tried examining myself, but the irritation seemed normal. I kept coming to the conclusion that ANYONE in this (or that) situation would be justifiably irritated.

I tried keeping my emotional buttons from being pressed. I put up all kinds of psychological warning signs:

"DO NOT Press THIS Button!"
"If you know what's best, DON'T depress!"
And even, "Please, Don't Press the Button."

Of course, that just seemed to bring more attention to the *button*. Even people that would not normally push the button tried it out just to see what would happen. I tried moving the button. This worked for a while, until they followed the wire and found the new location.

Suddenly, after much prayer, I heard myself tell someone, "You can knock at that door ALL you wish. I do not live there anymore." What I was referring to was the fact that I was in the process of moving my emotional baggage. That is when I realized that the button everybody was pushing was in fact the doorbell of my old emotional address.

Earlier, I thought the solution to the problem was to keep people from ringing the bell. But then they knocked on the door, called on the phone, and even climbed in the windows. The problem was not the button; it was my *address.* Any petition at the door required a response. I could not leave people on the porch; that seemed rude. Thus, I found myself constantly responding to other people's appeals for attention, so much so that I was at my wit's end. I decided I needed a change.

Not knowing where to go, I decided to move into temporary quarters until the Lord moved me. I remember telling a friend that, emotionally, I was living in a hotel for a while and wasn't giving the address out.

The suite God gave me was exquisite. I had a doorman who handled all visitors, and when I called anyone, the number that showed on their caller ID was the hotel switchboard. I had a "Do Not Disturb" order on my line. It was so nice, but I started wondering about the bill.

As time passed, more and more people realized I had moved and some even found my new location. The difference was that they could not *get to me*. This was when I realized the doorman was Jesus and the switchboard operator was the Holy Spirit. I had moved into the refuge called *SURRENDER*. He that dwell therein shall find PEACE.

This is where, with God's grace, I will remain.

Guess what; it isn't really a hotel.
It's a condo. (It's yours to own.)
Jesus paid the price, so there isn't even a mortgage.
Now,
Ain'-a that GOOD NEWS!

Occasionally, I accidently *drive* to the *old neighborhood*; however, as soon as I recognize that old familiar stress, I run back home!

(We Will Not Bow)

A Nebuchadnezzar Moment

Daniel 2:31-37

2001

GOD is in control! HIS word is truth!
He is the author of ALL facts!

And His is the ONLY opinion that CREATES facts!

As I sit to write the following story, I have no idea where it will lead me. I know, right now, I am standing in the shadow of a big obstacle that God must handle. The obstacle is not a person, nor is it a situation. The obstacle is MY response. I know that there really is no need to respond to a person's opinion. I always say, "Everyone has the God given right to be wrong", myself included. If opinions differ, so be it.

Trouble enters when someone wants their opinion treated as fact, or even worst, they want a fact to be treated as an opinion simply because they do not like the fact.

Opinions, though based on facts, do not become fact. They may be popular opinions. They may even lead to what may turn out to be a wise decision; but an opinion is an opinion. Your opinion sometimes changes as you add more facts. Opinions and conclusions differ between people and their emotional priorities, their likes and dislikes, or even a mood swing. Facts stand by themselves; they either are or are not.

Examples:
FACT: The house is on fire.
FACT: Fire burns.
FACT: People can get hurt returning into a burning building.
OPINION: People should not return into a home if it's on fire.
> I know, you may think the fourth one is a fact too, but if I add another fact the opinion may change.

> Added FACT: A six-month-old child was sleeping in the house while their parent was working in the yard.
> New OPINION: Now, a person is likely to return into a burning home! (See, the OPINION did change.)

I have learned to stand ON the facts and stand BY my opinions.

We tend to treat our opinions like facts. We gather and study our facts, stir them around a bit, and then come up with an opinion. We think our conclusion is a fact because it was based on facts. Most often, while stirring things around in our heads, we have unknowingly added *our stuff* to the mixture thereby changing the *flavor of the stew.*

FACT: God gave Nebuchadnezzar a dream about an image.
FACT: Nebuchadnezzar's Kingdom, Babylon, was great.
God's OPINION:
The head of gold was to represent Babylon's greatness. The fading of that greatness, as time passed, was represented by the breast and arms of silver, belly and thighs of brass, legs of iron, and feet of iron and clay. Daniel 2:36-43

Nebuchadnezzar's OPINION:
Nebuchadnezzar created an image of all gold to represent Babylon's never-ending greatness. He went so far as to think Babylon was great because of himself and his majesty.
Daniel 4:30

Like I said earlier, as facts are added, our opinions tend to change. That is why I say stand BY opinions. Standing too firmly ON opinions sometimes causes God to add facts and consequences. Too often, that is the only way He can mold our mindset into His will.

> Added FACT: Nebuchadnezzar lost his kingdom. Daniel 4:31
> Added FACT: Nebuchadnezzar became as a beast in the field. Daniel 4:33
> God's OPINION: I AM Jehovah. Exodus 6:1-3
> Nebuchadnezzar's NEW OPINION:
> Now I, Nebuchadnezzar, praise and extol and honor the King of heaven, all whose works are truth, and his ways judgment: and those that walk in pride He is able to abase.
>
> Daniel 4:37

It took Nebuchadnezzar seven years to see the foolishness of his pride. I hope this story line runs in prophetic time. Maybe, in this case, one year will equal one week. Seven weeks of living with Nebuchadnezzar's pride seems too long. The thought of seven years seems insufferable.

June

We constantly make decisions. We try to make sense of the facts we have before us. Sometimes they are pointing us in several directions, at the same time. Nevertheless, we study the facts as best we can, narrow our choices, and move forward.

FACT: I remarried almost two years ago.

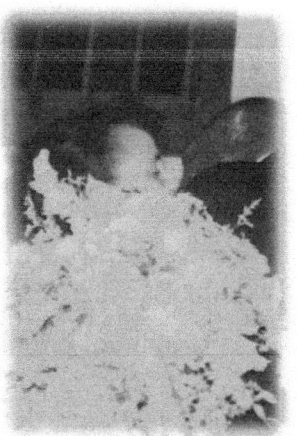

Right now, my husband is having a *moment*. He has dreamed GREAT dreams, and God is blessing him tremendously. The problem is that he does not like the way the blessings are coming. God has divided his *kingdom* and is trying to get him to see the big picture.

By this I mean that God has put people in his life that have parts of his dream. Together, the whole dream is already come to fruition. It is not completely up and running, but all the pieces are there like a puzzle, ready to be put into place when the time comes. Much like the statue in Nebuchadnezzar's time, one person has the head, the other the chest, one the loins, etc. The pieces are there, but the people must work together to bring the dream alive. On the other hand, my husband is dreaming of HIS statue of gold.

> We cause problems when we want the whole statue to be gold. If God has allotted us ONLY *the head,* how can we expect to bring the vision (He gave us) together outside of His perspective? Sometimes, the things we want are not the problem. Sometimes it's our ATTITUDE about the things we want that becomes the problem.

I feel my Nebuchadnezzar is constructing a statue of gold with dreams of bells ringing and advisors bowing at its feet. And consequently, he is creating a fiery furnace for those of us that are unwilling to bow. The moment is fast approaching where we will have to make our decision.

> Not to sound presumptuous, but I know who's in the fiery furnace. I figure the furnace is going to be the coolest place when all hell breaks loose.

Late June

AMAZING! One of the *advisors* finally got through to him—at least for the moment. For today, the light bulb turned on.

FACT: Marriage is a team effort of entangled unity. FACT: Marriage is not a business agreement between two individuals.

> I pray for prolonged understanding to come.
> Sometimes, it is not enough to be willing to help.
> Sometimes, the person needing help must be willing to be helped.

For now, my Nebuchadnezzar understands that he is the head and that there is a place in the vision for others to work. God's vision, in this case, is not to be achieved by any one person; in reality there are several people involved.

Early July

The first bell rang—Man, I blew that one!
I was so insistent not to bow that I found myself FIGHTING the people trying to get me into the fire. I even *threw stones* at the statue. The old nature rose and I utterly lost it!

It sounds so easy. We all want to say we will behave like the Hebrew boys. They simply stated, as a fact, "God has the power to save us. Whether he chooses to or not, He is still the God we serve." That is undeniably easier said than done.

When the heat of that fire starts *licking at your toes*, something fierce happens. Sorta' like the Hulk. (Comic's 1962)

> I felt a being swell up inside that burst out in a rage. Some would prefer to call it the devil; others have all kinds of nice ways to identify it as anything other than what/who it actually is. I saw it and recognized it well. I even knew it by name. It is better known as SELF! We sometimes want to add last names like Self-Awareness, Self-Pride, or even Self-Preservation. I see now—for sure, when facing the fiery furnace, *Self* will definitely be an obstacle.

> > The Hebrew boys simply stood. They did not make a big fuss or debate. When questioned they simply stated their belief. The Bible says nothing about them fighting the binding process.
> > Daniel 3:14-18

> > That was certainly the hardest part for me:
> > · Knowing God CAN save you; that is easy.
> > · Believing He WILLS to save you—easier.
> > · Trusting God TO save you?
> > You hope it's in His plan
> > · The binding—THAT is when you see how trusting you truly are.

In Daniel 3:21, the Bible says that the Jewish boys were bound in their hats, coats, hosiery, and other garments.
WAIT a minute:

> hat –helmet of,   coat –breastplate of,
> hosiery –feet shod with

God just did it again!
He never fails to give me an eye-popping twist…

Ephesians 6:11-20 tells the complete outfit for the fiery furnace.

Ephesians 6

11 Put on the **whole armour of God**, that ye may be able to *stand* against the wiles of the devil. **12** For we wrestle not with flesh and blood, but against principalities, against powers, against the rulers of the darkness of this world, against spiritual wickedness in high places. **13** Wherefore *take unto you the whole armour of God*, that ye may be able to withstand the evil day, and having done all, to stand. **14** *Stand therefore*, having your **loins girt** about with truth, and having the **breastplate** of righteousness; **15** And your **feet shod** with the preparation of the gospel of peace; **16** Above all, taking the **shield** of Faith, wherewith ye shall be able to quench all the fiery darts of the wicked. **17** And take the **helmet** of salvation, and the **sword** of the Spirit, which is the word of God. **18** Praying always with all prayer of supplication in the Spirit and watching thereunto with all perseverance and supplication for all saints; **19** And for me, that utterance may be given unto me, that I may open my mouth boldly, to make known the mystery of the gospel, **20** For which I am **an ambassador in bonds**: that therein I may speak boldly, as I ought to speak.

So, I will dust off and settle down into the things God has put before me to do. To help strengthen my walk, I will make the changes He has shown me. God has given me my orders—Just STAND.

Please, excuse me a while. I need to take off my Hulk costume and get dressed, in the *proper attire*.

Now, as darts of false guilt and self-doubt are hurled my way, I will continue to stand, dressed in the full armor of God!

Mid July

A thought, to digest:

The fact that the boys went INTO the furnace without being burnt was the miracle that caught Nebuchadnezzar's eye. He didn't see Christ until AFTER the boys were in the fire. I don't know if I like that.

Think about it— watching the boys IN the furnace walking amongst the flames is when Nebuchadnezzar noticed Christ in there with them. Daniel 3:24 – 25

Does that mean that God will not show-up until I am IN the fire? That is a scary thought! Now that I know how hard it is to let myself be thrown into *fire*, it is even more difficult.

Late July

The Lord has truly blessed! One of the things I feared (and there are several), has come to be a simple test of faithfulness.

I found myself swimming downstream in a financial *river*. This was not a pleasure trip—I had fallen in, and the *water* was well over my head. I told my mom that I had been swimming so hard and so long, without coming up for air, that I did not notice that God had slipped me a *diver's mask* and *air tank*.

Praise God!

By the time I tried to *come up for air*, I was *in so deep*, I would have gotten *the bends* if I came up too quickly. I had finally gotten used to the rules, of the *water*, and thought I would eventually be able to make my way to the *riverbank*.

Suddenly, the financial *river* came to an end with nothing but a gigantic *waterfall* ahead of me, and I was not yet able to swim to the shores. Because of the drive of the current, I had to go forward. Just as I reached the *falls*, I started reminding God of his promises.

We all know Who was reminding who:
Bring ye all the tithes into the storehouse and prove me now herewith, saith the Lord of hosts, if I will not open the windows of heaven and pour you out a blessing, that there shall not be room enough to receive it.

Malachi 3:10

Give and it shall be given unto you; good measure, pressed down, SHAKEN together, and overflowing.

Luke 6:38

Side thought:
Have you ever poured flour into a container? When you have a little more left, you shake the container to make some more room. Shake a little then add a little; shake a little more and add a little more— until all the flour is in or there is just no more room in the container.

God shakes our container, so as not to waste any space, and then continues to POUR. He does not trickle His blessings; so as not to waste any. God just shakes us down and POURS. His blessings do not go to waste, and they do not run out. When we are in His will, what overflows from our container flows directly into the need of someone else.

Back to the *waterfalls*:
God, let me go over. He did not stop the flow. Instead of saving me FROM the river, He saved me IN the river. Remember the air tank He slipped me earlier? When

God connects you to a saving device, strap in and hold on tightly. That same air tank did something totally unexpected. Out of nowhere, it became a parachute. Instead of God slowing the waterfall, He slowed MY fall!

I landed, still in the river, and I have to swim a while. But wearing God's *Life Jacket* that doubles as an air tank, which becomes a parachute when needed, makes the trip a whole lot less worrisome.

And you thought James Bond
was the only one with stuff like that!
My God is the author of ALL that is Good!
HALLELUIA!

I realize you are not hearing much about Nebuchadnezzar right now. God is working on that part of the story. I can only write about the side I am living. Isn't it miraculous how God has billions of story lines going at one time and weaves them in and out of each other? All the while He promises, "Be ye confident of this very thing, that he which hath begun a good work will perform it until the day of Jesus Christ." Philippians 1:6

August

Years ago, my sons used to squabble:
It's not fair!!!!!
> **It's NOT Fair!!!!**
> > **It just ain't fair!!!**

You gave him more ice cream than you gave me.
> That's not fair!

You helped him rake the yard, but you won't help me!
> Not fair!

Why can't I go?   That's not fair!
Why did he get to stay up?   That's not fair!
How come I have to wash dishes this week?   That's not fair!

I used to tell my sons ALL THE TIME,
> "Life ISN'T fair! Get over it!"

This time it was ME. I was literally pacing the floor.

"That's not fair!   No way!   God, that's just not fair!"
"I paid my tithes and gave my offering!   That's not fair!"
"You're supposed to rain down the blessings."
"Why do I have to pay it? I didn't do it— That's not fair!"

God replied: **"Life's NOT fair! Get over it!"**
"Do you deserve the job you have? Did you do anything for
that bonus you just received? Which of the blessings you've
been telling people about, did you earn? Why do I bless you,
with these things, and not someone else? Are you any better
than they?"
"Life ISN'T fair and be glad of it."
"Now pay the thing and get over it!"
"To whom much is given, much is required!"

Luke 12:48

The boys did not always know my reasons for handling
situations the way I did; but **I** always knew. So, that is why this
particular chastisement made me laugh. Even though you may
have a problem with the thought of God speaking so bluntly,
God knows me and gave me a dose of my own medicine. I had
to literally laugh-out-loud.

I was planning a trip to go halfway around the word in the next
few weeks. I watched God move, in such mighty ways, to bring
the pieces together, I thought He had blessed me with the trip
to allow things to settle down after **I** won the battle. Of course,
I would win— I pay my tithes and return my offerings! Little
did I know He was getting me *out of Dodge*, all right. But, not
to avoid trouble; instead, He was removing me so I would not
START any trouble. In fact, He was sending me, literally,
halfway around the world to cool off.

God dealt with me on the tithe issue too:

He said, "You certainly don't want to go down that road! Do you think your tithe is a bribe? Am I to be bought? – Again, didn't I keep your lights turned on? If I can pay one bill, I most certainly can pay another. If I want to pay it THROUGH you, I will!"

That revelation came quickly, and I heeded just as quickly. Again, the fire had gotten hot, and I was feeling bound up in my circumstances, but this time, by submitting and listening, God was able to work.

Early September

What, a wonderful vacation! Not that I wanted to travel alone, but I learned a while back that you should enjoy your own company. (I do!) I was visiting my youngest son that was stationed in Yokosuka, Japan and was on a tight shoestring budget. My son and some of his shipmates rented a house located just a few subway stops from the Naval Base and offered me a bedroom during my stay. This trip was a blessing, tailor-made for me!

The guys welcomed a visiting mom (especially one that liked washing dishes), so I became Mom to a houseful of sailors. "Momma on deck!"[32] was the call when I came downstairs in the morning. We ALL had a ball! The weather was just right, and I got to experience living outside of the tourist-y areas. The experience was utterly refreshing. Even my mix-up on the subway turned into a wonderful sight-seeing tour.

It took a couple of escorted excursions before I dared to venture out alone among the non-English speaking public. By that time, I had enough basic skills to count money, make telephone calls, and read the maps.

---

[32] which translates: no cursing and other *sailor* stuff

When I got lost, it was scary AND exhilarating at the same time. Praying all the way, I decided to enjoy the ride. Three hours and two rolls of film later, I  eventually reached my destination.

For the mere cost of a subway ticket, I traveled hundreds of miles and saw several cities as well as numerous rural areas. Quite a few times I got off the subway and stood on the platform to see the cities and watch people as they went along their daily routines. A prepared tour would have never fit in my budget.

I cherished the prospect of encountering so many experiences in Japan: shopping, site seeing, and spending time with my son. Even getting lost was a growth opportunity that bolstered a better insight towards non-English speaking foreigners visiting the USA. AND the adventure let me do what I love to do; see everyday people living their daily lives, instead of the fake lifestyles so often depicted in tourist areas.

God blessed me tremendously! I saw so much, learned so much, enjoyed so much, and I was taken so far out of my element that I had no choice but to cool off.

Late September

...Back home and in the thick of things:

God, I do not understand. I'm telling the truth. Is everybody lying or has satan (with a small s) deceived them? Am I stupid for continuing to stand here? I feel so alone. Why is everybody mad at ME?

Let me look back over it again:
Yes, I could have handled things differently, but I have admitted that. My problem is that everyone is pointing to me. No one seems to be telling HIM that he is wrong.

I'm just standing here. I feel so alone—but,
Thou art with me. Thy rod and thy staff shall comfort me.
Psalms 23:4

Why are the advisors angry and annoyed with me? I'm simply stating the truth. When will You, God, rise up in my behalf? The more he tells it his way, the more people fall for his illusion.

But right now, in all honesty I feel as if I'm standing against the world. I feel so frustrated and alone. Why shouldn't I be angry? Everyone believes a lie. Again, I ask, "When will you rise up?" I want vindication! I know what I'm saying is right. Why is there no one who understands? I know you have my back, but what kind of witness am I when everyone seems to be deceived. I cannot even speak out on my behalf because then THAT is misinterpreted. Has satan pulled a cloud of darkness over their understanding? – I feel so bound u—p...

Oh my God! The story—I forgot all about it!
Go *get the laptop!*

> The music was played, and the Hebrew boys did not bow. THEN, when Nebuchadnezzar brought them forward, they were given a SECOND chance. Though I knew it in theory, I had not brought it to my conscious thinking that there were TWO commands to bow in the storyline. It was after they were given a SECOND chance to bow that the boys were bound.

Before, what I thought was binding was just the music playing. Yes, while standing firm was hard to do, I realize now that I was not bound earlier because I could move. I could also talk; now I see the difference. Earlier, I was feeling the pressure of standing, ill equipped, against the tide of fear and pressure. THAT time, I did not have on my armor and the binding had not even started.

Now, I see what is good about being bound. You CAN'T move, which is handy because then, while remaining in God's will, you cannot make a WRONG move. Looking back, I see that binding started when the time for talking was over. At that point, there was nothing else to be said. So, in all intents and purposes, I am gagged too. So, here I stand bound and gagged. God, you've been telling me for a week or so, *Just walk with the Spirit.* You haven't even had to raise your voice this time. You've been able to guide me.

The Lord is my Shepherd. I shall not want.
Thank You Lord! Selah!

God speaks:
Don't worry. There are people watching that you do not even know about. Just stand! Nebuchadnezzar just doesn't understand it yet— He WILL know I Am— Just stand.

~.~.~.~.~.~.~.~.~.~

God be praised!!!
He gave me this story months ago. Only through IT could I ever understand what has been happening.

> I AM in a valley among the *nobles.* That is why everyone around me seems to be falling for the deceit that has been *orchestrated.* I feel *bound up* because I can neither act nor speak on my behalf. I did not even feel the binding process. I only noticed when I could no longer move.

My God, you warned me, *Just Stand*. That is amazing to me. God has been preparing me for this moment before I could even imagine it would happen. He even gave me a rest break (the vacation in Japan) to give me the second wind for this round.

> He maketh me lie down in green pastures;
> He leadeth me beside still waters.
> He RESTORETH my soul. Psalms 23: 2-3

Early October

DRAMA.! Most people think that WOMEN are dramatic.
Picture Nebuchadnezzar's scene: hundreds, if not thousands, of princes, governors, captains, treasurers, counselors, and sheriffs—nobleman from the providences of Babylon—standing out in a large field. They have come to worship, dressed in their native formal dress attire of beautiful colors and garbs.

> It is my understanding that during that period in history, Babylon had conquered many nations. The nobles of these conquered cities were usually taken back to Babylon and indoctrinated, if possible, into Babylonian leadership. Instead of stripping the people of all their customs and beliefs, they were allowed to maintain the traditions that did not take away from the Babylonian culture or override any of the Babylonian laws. In this case, the fiery furnace was for those nobles unwilling to *go with the* Babylonian *flow*.

Thus, the dramatic scene out in the plains: these captive dignitaries out in the Plains of Dura, in the province of Babylon, mandated to worship a statue representing the greatness of Babylon. The sun shining brightly with beaming radiance from the gigantic golden statue erected there. An orchestra on hand to play music at the bidding of the king. The king's throne probably positioned on the top of a tall, majestic platform, and a large furnace erected a little ways off. Alongside the furnace—a mountain of coal.

The King stands overlooking the people gathered to worship him and his kingdom. Standing in front of his throne, he slowly raises his scepter, and the orchestra starts playing music. Melodious harp and flute sounds ring throughout the plains. As the music rises, like a mighty ocean tide, people begin a wave of bowing. It starts from the front and works its way to the back. Even beyond what the eye can see, a wave of people bowing to worship the golden image that Nebuchadnezzar had constructed. How much more dramatic can you get?

Never underestimate the drama of a proud man with a dream!

I look back at the beginning of this story. Though I wrote it several months ago, it was as if I just wrote it today. But then I realize that Nebuchadnezzar did not change during the playing of the music, nor did he change when the boys were bound. He did not even soften as the guards heated up the furnace. Seeing men under his charge drop dead at the heat of the furnace did not sway him either. Only when he saw the boys walking with Jesus in the midst of the fire did his heart get pierced.
Again, God Speaks,
Be Still! Remember— I said, 'Just Stand!'

Late October

If making someone else feel insignificant is your means to greatness, then your greatness has become insignificant.

GAP - (Gospel According to Pam!)

Let me take a short side trip and talk a little about Joseph and his brothers for a moment. We'll get back to Nebuchadnezzar on the other side of this *barn*; sometimes you *see* more on the scenic route.

In Genesis 37, when Joseph spoke of HIS dream, his brothers told him that they would NEVER bow to him:

"Who do you think you are having dreams of us bowing to you?" Gen. 37:8 They decided to strip him of his dignity (his coat of colors) and sold him into slavery. Gen. 37:23-28

What in the world does that have to do with Nebuchadnezzar? Nebuchadnezzar, like Joseph's brothers, thought he was greater than the dream God gave.

> Just like Joseph's brothers tried to make Joseph and his dream insignificant, Nebuchadnezzar thought he could make the Hebrew boys insignificant as well. In his pride, he was going to use them to show his greatness. That's when God stepped in— literally.

Be Careful—
If YOUR dream discounts the dream that God has given the people around you, you should check to see if your pride has distorted your perspective.

> *Be ye careful of the seeds you sow;*
> *you may have to eat humble pie made from the fruit thereof.*
> **GAP**

Late November
Again, I digress from the main storyline; but I promise—this is an essential trip around a worthy barn.

> *There is nothing worse than trying to get a serious game of chess going with distracted people.*

My favorite board game is chess. I love to play a fast friendly game. I like to play even though I seldom win. I don't ever remember playing against a woman and men usually play a deeper strategy than I. So, instead of trying to win, my goal is to give my opponent a good run for their money. My posture is always: *You will probably win, but I bet you can't do it in less than 15-20 minutes.* The guys that sit down thinking, *I'll blow her out the water* are the ones I usually beat.

When I learned chess, I was taught several principles of strategy:

1) Protect in threes. (Protect one piece 3 ways.)
2) When attacked from one direction—Castle.[33]
3) Do not lead with pieces you can't afford to lose.
4) A properly placed pawn is as mighty as a queen.
5) Winning the battle does not always win the war.
6) Watch for your opponent's next few moves.
7) Note how far your opponent is from their attack.
8) Be closer to your attack… or prepare for theirs.
9) It is not how many pieces you have that count.
10) It's the power of the pieces and their clever use.
11) Never move easily into a corner.
12) Never give up—Make your opponent think!
13) Play each move all the way to the end.

For years, I lived by these rules; an offshoot of Shakespeare's *All the world is a* –chess game. These rules worked well. Life became a game to be played. I was not going to win all the time, but I wanted to play it well. I did not mind losing a few battles as long as I gave my opponent a good game.

Some opponent's strategy was to strip all my power. Other opponents would leave my powerful pieces in place but block them so they couldn't help. Both strategies usually gave my opponents control of the board! These were the most popular strategies, but of course there were many others. That was half the fun— figuring out their strategy and making countermoves at the same time.

A few years back, on my job, I was having a lot of difficulty, because I had allowed the *game* to make me aggressively defensive. I was under attack, and I

---

[33] Castling is a strategic chess move that quickly relocates your King.

felt they were trying to back me into a corner. I mentally sat down to the board and said, *Okay! Let's Play!* I literally told a co-worker, "If you don't want to play, get away from the table. The game is chess, not checkers!" I prepared for the battle, anticipated their moves, protected my power, decided which pieces were expendable, and was ready to play. I dug in deep and got ready for war!

The Lord, through my sister, told me to stop the games. I had to stop looking at people as the opponent. Satan is the opponent. Though I may not have liked what they were doing, I had to look at them as my team members. I could not judge them to be against me; that was God's call to make. I only needed to know "God be for me!" Romans 8:31 So, at that point, I made a conscious effort to leave the games behind.

Every now and then, before I notice, I get pulled into a game and play a while before I catch myself. But as soon as I do notice, I endeavor to quit. Most of the time, I can tell when someone is trying to *get a game going*. I see them tote the board into the room, look for a freed table, start to set up the pieces, and I even watch them move around the room, asking other people *to play*.

Most board games are competitive and usually yield only one winner. Chess is no different. People that *play* life as a board game generally yield win/lose situations. They treat others as the advisory and fight to win every time. Leaving the chess game allowed me to mentality look for win/win solutions instead.

Today, I saw my husband come in wanting to *get a game going*! He was packed and ready. He set the board and was working the room for players. Seeing the inevitable (and tired of the game), I internally cried out, *Lord, when I see them coming, what is there to do?*

God said, "Stop watching! You are watching their every move from the time they enter the room. From their point of view, you look interested. You are presenting yourself as someone *looking to play*! Find some other focus!—Start *serving ice cream*!"

To my surprise, as my husband approached, I scooped up a heap of kindness and literally said, "Want some ice cream, honey? I'm not, playing chess tonight." He looked at me like I was crazy, but it broke his concentration and I started talking about something else.

December
Stop the Madness!
I have not only stopped playing the game, but I have refused to participate in the drama, as well. I'm tired!

The Lord has given me a whole new viewpoint.
1. Nebuchadnezzar only controlled the APPEARANCE of his drama. He prepared the scene: The fiery furnace, the orchestra, the command to attend and worship, the design of the image—in general all the things out on the plains of Dura. God was in control of the outcome!

2. The real issue was not who would bow. That became an issue only as the nobles chose to participate. As God showed, through the Hebrew boys, when the participants refused to participate, THEIR drama ended.

3. The real issue was the fact that Nebuchadnezzar had the audacity and purposeful false pride, to misrepresent the dream that God had given him. God unfolded the future to Nebuchadnezzar and Nebuchadnezzar had the nerve to call himself able to rewrite it.

We hear nothing else about the image on the plains after God delivered the Hebrew boys. We do, however, continue to read about God's workings in Nebuchadnezzar's life; trying to deal with him and his issues of false pride.

Daniel 4:30-32; 34

I have finally learned what the Hebrew boys knew all along.

The DRAMA is not the issue.
When I refuse to participate in the drama, I allow the Lord to handle the real issue.

January

Snow has fallen, melted, and fallen again. This is the beginning of the seventh month. It did not take seven years. Praise God!

> In reality, it did not have to take seven months. I retarded the unfolding because of my side trips and issues. I never had to go into a fiery furnace. All I had to do was learn to STAND. God is in ultimate control of those who dare to think themselves in control! Furthermore, even more importantly (to me) is that God is also in control of those who choose to stand despite the drama!

God will continue to deal with my husband and his issues. As for me and this drama,

> It is finished! John 19:30

> Jesus hung on the cross to pay the price, rose in victory to open the way.

> God is, truly, amazing!

PS: As I saved this document, I noticed the date:
> Today is January 1rst.

A new year, basis for a new page and a fresh slate.

Selah!

The Gospel of the Hedges

2002

In previous stories, I mentioned the line of evergreen trees that form a hedge-like fringe along the side of my home. Though we trim them regularly, we have not topped-them-off for several years. Now, they stand about fourteen feet tall. It is November and my sons, Timothy and Kienen (who are now young men), came over to help prune the trees and clean-up the yard.

Though the treetops were alive and healthy, we decided to cut a few feet off the tops, bringing the trees down to about eight feet tall. This allows us to stand on the ground and use the pole cutter to trim them. It was a major undertaking that took three days, about eight hours each day.

As we were working, one son jokingly reminded me that fire was an option. I said, "Over my dead body!" We all paused, looked at each other, and burst out in laughter!

> I was the first to speak of the scene at the funeral. As my casket was being lowered into the ground. Suddenly, people standing around would be astonished to hear my sons scream, "FIRE!". Some would say, "Are they having a gun salute?" Others would say, "I thought she was a Christian woman. It is such a shame her sons think she is going to burn." Only the neighbors would know—those trees are HISTORY!

They assured me they would respect my love for my trees. They would leave them up no less than two weeks. I told them that the problem with them knowing God's Word is that I could not threaten to come back and haunt them. Eccl 9:5

> That scene is still a cherished laughing good memory!

As we finished up the hard days' labor, I stopped to share *Life Lesson #782*. We make up the numbers as we go; it is just our way of saying remember this:

- Sometimes, just before our *fall*, God needs to shape us up. If we are getting too *big*, He may have to cut us down a bit so that we are manageable from the ground.

- We need to make sure all cuttings are removed. The enzyme of negativity, secreted by the *disconnected clippings*, can kill even that which is connected.

- God wants to prune ALL our dead limbs; the energy wasted trying to bring life into them can kill a tree.

- When God trims your tree, sometimes He may have to cut deep simply because He is giving you room to grow back. He does not want your new growth to impede those coming down the *sidewalk*.

Have you ever had one of those moments when you pat yourself on the back and say, "Oh what a wonderfully wise parent I am?" What usually happens next? For me, something usually happens to remind me who I really am.

Timothy, referring to the pruning as cutting away unhealthy relationships, stated that maybe this was a lesson **I** needed to apply.

God quickly corrected the definition. I know it was God because I had no answer and had drawn a complete blank! I heard these words coming from my mouth:

"Point— Counter Point" and continued,

- "We stand as individual trees before God, and together, we form a hedge. The trimming I was speaking of is a trimming of an individual's character.

- God says, in marriage, the two become one. He means the two trees become one hedge. The pruning is a trimming away of old habits, insecurities, and such.

- Each person God puts in our lives is an individual tree unto himself or herself. They are fully accountable to God for themselves. If God removes them, He will *uproot* them. Only God can make the decision who is dead wood, and He will deal with each tree separately. But be ye sure, God WILL *cast out* dead wood, like kindling for fire, at the second death. Rev 20:12-14

- As a Melted Family, we all stand as a unit. Just like these trees stand in the hedge, each individually accountable, before God; yet, connected as a hedge intermingling and interacting; supporting and securing."

The way the world thinks is to just cut down that old tree that *ain't acting right!* Well, as an *Old Tree* myself, I prefer to prune and trim.

"Note:

The older the tree....

Though we may be a bit wider....

We make the better shade!"

TOO MUCH STUFF!

2003

I felt like life was closing in; there was no room. Every emotional corner I had was piled with STUFF. There was stuff everywhere! I started examining it and realized most of it was not mine. It belonged to all kinds of people: friends, family, neighbors, coworkers, bosses, and even church members.

I started sorting through each pile. As fast as I would get some stuff "sorted out", there was someone from somewhere dropping another pile. I looked up and noticed the doorways. All around my personal space were doorways. The piles were not the problem; I needed to control those doorways. I decided to install some DOORS!

I recently hung doors to control the flow of *stuff* being dumped into my emotional space. Immediately, when the doors went up, I started hearing outcries of indignation: "How dare you be so controlling?" "Who put you in charge?" "Who gave you authority to install doors?" I was sure I was right; after all, it was MY *space*!

I needed to ask someone—but before I picked up the telephone, I literally started counting the doors. I got to fifteen, became overwhelmed, and just estimated the total to be about twenty. Behind each of the doors were other people and their—*stuff*!

I called my pastor and talked about my *space*: "I feel like I'm sitting in the middle of a room. Surrounding the room, on all four walls, are doors." I asked, "Do I need to remove the doors? Are they too controlling?"

Pastor asked an interesting question, "What are the doors?" I had not thought of that. After a moment, I realized, "Boundaries—The doors are personal boundaries." None of the doors were locked and anyone could enter; I did not even require them to knock. The only new dictate was that their *stuff* must stay on the other side of their door unless I allowed it in.

Now that I am cleaning *my room* and handling *my stuff*, I am by the same token returning *piles* to their initial owners.

Like an announcement at a discount department store an hour before closing time, "All departments need to pick up items from the customer service desk!" "Let's work together so we can get out of here on time." I broadcasted my new philosophy; and, after the free-will *pickups* were finished, I personally returned the leftover unclaimed *stuff* to the proper *departments*.

Once I cleared away the piles, it became easier to define *my stuff* in what was left. Now, if someone comes in wearing their *stuff* like a cheap monkey suit, I ask them to leave. I am too tired, too stressed, and I'm enjoying my recently found peace way too much to engage in other people's foolishness and issues. They can return at any time. They just need to leave their junk on the other side of the door. Right now, I am working on my own *stuff*.

I spoke to my sister, Jackie, about my doors. She asked me about doorknobs, "The door on which Jesus knocks", she said, "opens from our side. Jesus' side does not have a knob. We must let Him in. What about your doors?" I replied without a second thought, almost in a panic, "Oh, no! I have knobs— there ARE knobs on both sides of the doors, I need the KNOBS! My goal is to keep myself from putting on LOCKS!"

My son, Timothy, came in one day wearing a furry suit. I won't classify it as monkey or ape; I will just say furry. It surprised him when I made him check it at the door. There was a hook, right there on his side of the door, just a waitin'.

It took a moment (and a hang-up of the phone) to get him to realize the new rules. I let him cool a minute and called him back. He asked me if I was treating everyone this way. I quickly replied, "Yes. I was not trying to be rude; I was simply refusing to accept the bundle you were trying to drop off." Then he said, "Well, maybe you need to check yourself. You told me that when I think everybody else has a problem, I need to check myself!" This was true; I did say that! I HAD checked myself, and I found a solution for the problem—the doors.

My response was, "Just because a person has a load to drop doesn't mean they get to drop it in MY space; I do not see a problem with that. It's just good *housekeeping*."

In the past, when I complained, as people left unaccompanied baggage in *my room*, they laid a guilt trip with comments like, "Don't be so controlling", which usually led to me becoming out of control. Now, I realize that there is nothing wrong with me controlling the access of out-of-control people.

So, in an effort to help others become accountable for their *stuff*, and in response to attempts to leave me holding their *bag*, let me tell everybody *where they can put their stuff*—
JESUS says:

Bring your burdens to HIM
and HE will give you rest.
His yoke is easy, and His burden is light.

Matt 11:28-29

Maintenance Required

2004

*There is a major difference in tripping, falling, and slipping. I
have tripped many times and felt myself regroup in mid-air as I
grabbed something or someone, re-gained my composure, and
then landed with little out of place. I have similarly fallen.
There too, I found myself in mid-air twisting into a good
landing position. In both cases, things seemed to move in slow
motion. Slipping on ice was a whole new ball of wax. Time
seemed to fast-forward; there was absolutely no time for
thought. First, I was standing; then I was stretched out on the
pavement, seeing stars. The only conscious thought I had
between standing and landing, was the feeling of "POP!" in
my ankle.*

I was taking the trash out when I slipped. I made it back into
the house by reminding myself that I was outside in the freeze
of winter, without a coat, where no one would see me for hours.
I convinced myself it was just a bad sprain and slowly walked
up the yard and climbed the backstairs. I plopped myself down,
at the kitchen table, right inside the back door; then, lifted my
foot into one of the chairs and paused to watch all the pretty
white stars circling the room.

> I always thought the old saying *seeing stars* was an
> exaggeration or old-time joke with misremembered
> meanings. Nope! It is true; I in fact saw stars circling
> my head when I made it into the house; the telephone
> was on the wall right above them.

I called my husband, William, who made it home as quickly as
he could. We tried to maneuver with crutches to no avail, so he
called an ambulance. When they arrived, I calmly gave them
the information they needed. Because of my demeanor, they
were totally convinced I had nothing more than a bad sprain.

They assured me if anything were broken, I would not be sitting and chatting like I was. William, on the other hand, knowing me better, insisted they take me in the ambulance. He later said he could tell by my eyes something was wrong, and he did not want me going into shock while he was trying to drive.

During triage at the hospital, all of a sudden, for no reason, I felt myself start to shake to the point that I had to hold my hands to maintain any resemblance of composure. Only I knew that the tears streaming down my face were not from pain; they just kept coming. The emergency room staff still did not notice the change. I told an attendant that I felt like I was having a panic attack and she said, "No, you are way too calm." Inside, I was screaming and scared. Without realizing it, I had kicked into survival mode and was unconsciously hiding the severity of my injury. That is until they took x-rays. I did not realize it at that time, but in hindsight, after the x-rays revealed the three breaks, suddenly, they treated me with kit-gloves. I even got a blanket.

All patched up, pins in place, and surgery finished I was back at home to heal. At first the downtime seemed like a blessing. It was a good chance for me to slow down and a good time for others to learn to take the lead. While I tried to use this period of immobilization as an opportunity to learn to communicate clearly and completely, it absolutely proved to be an opportunity for others to learn to listen and remember details.

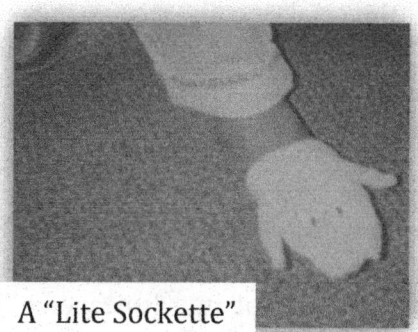
A "Lite Sockette"

Like a saucer spinning on a stick, family and friends would get me spinning, and I could spin a good while on my own before I needed any more help.

I relinquished the S from my Superwoman costume quickly and easily. I was surprised when the world did not come to the crashing holt that I thought it would. Instead, it shifted gently, rolled off my shoulders, and turned back onto its own axis; the populace was none the wiser. Maybe there was something in that for me to learn.

As of today, I've been close to helpless in an ankle cast for almost four weeks. The first two weeks weren't too bad. That period allowed me to catch-up on paperwork, spreadsheets, and databases. I even created some "*lite-sockettes*" to keep my toes warm while wearing my  cast. I had craft and office supplies at arms' reach beside my bed. We put a mini refrigerator in the bedroom and stocked it with juices, water, soy milk, and ice packs. So, I was quite the little camper.

Now, weeks later, I am still here still unable to do it, make it, or even get anything outside of this room. This is totally foreign to my family. Because of my faith, they have never seen me give in to helplessness. I have come to realize that in trying to keep their world secure, I robbed them of the knowledge of how GOD was holding things together—not Mommy.

Going back many years, I remember Kienen (my middle son) standing in the kitchen, eating a popsicle. I was watching a small television that was sitting in one of the kitchen chairs as I cooked. Kienen moved over the TV while licking his Popsicle. When I told him to move because it may drip into the TV, he, in the innocence of his seven or eight years, with absolutely no understanding of the meaning of what he was saying, replied, "That's okay. You'll just open it up and fix it." It felt good at the time that he was so confident in his mommy. But now I see, it would have been better if his gut-level response had been, "That's ok, Mommy. God will help you fix it."

In my heart I knew God was my strength; but my calm confident demeanor gave the impression that I was the conqueror. Many people saw my faith as ego and my assurance as conceit. Even though I was always talking about God's blessings and His faithfulness, by hiding my fears and weaknesses, I believe I may have hid some of God's glory. *I can do ALL things through Christ that strengtheneth me!* [34] has been my banner, but people took it as cliché when I gave God the Glory.

For the last couple of years, I have complained about caring for the needs of my family and none of them returning to *fill my cup*. But now I see that unless my family can SEE my weaknesses, they cannot support me. My *being strong through it all* seems to have been a disadvantage for all of us.

Back when my sons were in their teens, I talked to them about my being a ladder helping them climb *the wall*. We talked about my fear that they would get over to the other side and walk off, leaving me behind used, worn, and on the outside, unable to climb. I told them, "Please, don't drag me over the wall. Go find the door, open it from the inside, and let me walk in." I know they are willing; I just need to learn to SHOW my wear and tear.

I think that over the years it has been established that I will *get it done*. Everyone knows it is Christ in me, but few realize how

---

[34] Philippians 4:13

little of it is me. As a result, when Christ is moving them to help, people seldom see my need.

I need you –

You need me.
We're all part of God's body.
It is His will that EVERY need be supplied.
You are important to me!
I need YOU to survive!

(Walker 2005)

Seldom, do we get over the hump on our own. Though God is always lifting us from above, He still wants us to do our part and climb. He provides us with people to help, serving as our ladders, ropes, hooks, and other apparatus.

In God's plan, well maintained equipment doesn't feel used; it enjoys the challenge of being needed!

Things That Make You Go Hummm
2005—2006

Periodically, God speaks to me through stories and allegories. Usually, He speaks to me through personal experiences. Sometimes He only gives me a kernel of wisdom. However, God's kernels can be so rich with meaning that I have a feast. I share these thoughts, below, because I dare not eat alone.

Preserver vs. Swimmer

2005

A young swimmer sees a drowning man. He cannot throw the life preserver out far enough. He must think fast, and he is alone.

The young swimmer knows he is strong enough to swim out to the drowning man, so he heads out to him. He carries a life preserver with him. When he reaches the man in trouble, the young man grabs the drowning man's hands, trying to get him to latch onto the preserver. Instead, the drowning man panics and grabs the young swimmer in a chokehold around his neck.

The young swimmer remembers what he learned in swimming class: he will be drowned, along with the other man, if he lets that man's fear pull him down. He breaks free and moves away. The young man then calms the other man and talks him into grabbing the preserver, now positioned between them, at the drowning man's fingertips. Only in this way is the young swimmer in a true *saving position*.

Now, it is up to the drowning man. He must CHOOSE to grab the life preserver if he wants to be saved.

Some people's burdens are not for us to bear; it is our job to bring them into reach of the *Life Preserver*.

Heart-too-Hard (vs. Heart-to-Heart)

It is dumfounding! The evil justified by a heart waxed cold.

Birds of a Feather

Like a mother bird, sometimes we chew the *meat* of the Word, only to regurgitate it later into someone else's life.

Sometimes we are the hen.
Sometimes we are the hatchling.

How can a man lead a strong woman?

It is as easy as flying a kite. He lets her sore, guiding her away from the dangers of *trees* and *wires*. Occasionally he may have to pull against the wind to keep her safe, which may cause some tension, but he is always mindful not to break the connection. He keeps her grounded.

Chosen   2006

Being "Chosen by God" for something does not mean that you are perfect for it. It means that IN GOD, you are perfect for it. If you chose to leave God's will, you leave the perfection God has intended.

If He knows the beginning from the end, why did God choose you for something when He knew you would not follow Him to the end of it? Did God make a mistake in choosing you? No, God does not make mistakes—God gives us the opportunity for His perfection. We make decisions that move us into, or out of, His will and choosing! That is the meaning of free will; we get to CHOOSE to remain chosen.

Want IT?

Weigh IT… Pray IT! Say IT….

Handle IT!

'Tis true at 18....20....21....25......and even 30
*By 50 you should be teaching **it**!*

*First let's talk about **it**.* (Your Temple)
    If **it** ain't been washed, brushed, or combed TODAY,
    with soap, gel, or paste, then the answer is   NO!
      It's okay.
          I'm just running around the corner   NO!
      It's okay. No one will notice
          I can just throw on a hat;   NO!
      It's okay.
          I don't have time to shower   NO!
      I'll be okay with a little cologne   NO! NO! NO!
      I don't smell **it,** I'm okay   NO!

    If you cannot remember the last time a professional has
    checked **it**, then the answer is... ....   YES!
      I have no symptoms
          do I really need to go?   YES!
      I don't have money to waste
          do I really need to go?   YES!
      I brush every day
          do I really need to go?   YES!
      Last time it was nothing
          do I really need to go?   YES! YES! YES!

   It is mine; I can do as I please with **it**.
      The answer is:
   It's been given to you to Glorify YOUR God! III John 1:2

*Next, let's talk about **it**.* (Your Finances and Resources)
    Do you NEED to buy **it** or want to buy **it**?
    Can you afford **it**?
    Did your lack of planning turn **it** into an emergency?

How much of **it** is for selfish pride?

It is mine! I worked hard for **it**! I can do as I please with **it**.
   The answer is:
It's been given to you to Glorify YOUR God! Luke 16:10-13

Now, let's talk about it. (Your Time)
   If you check **it**, you are less likely to repeat **it**.
   Plan **it** and account for every need.
   Before you sign **it**, commit to the completed end.

It is mine! I'm grown! I can do as I please with **it**.
   The answer is:
It's been given to you to Glorify YOUR God! Ecc. 9:10, 12

Finally, let's talk about it. (Your Salvation)
   I've heard **it** all my life.
   What is in **it** for me?
   Why can't I do **it** my way?

Jesus paid for **it**,
   all you need do is claim **it**.

The answer is YES!
I've done so much stuff. Does Jesus still want me?
                                                          YES!
I've done so much stuff. Can I truly change my life?   YES!
I've done so much stuff. Is Christianity fun?   YES! YES!

It is mine; I can do as I please with **it**!
   The answer is:
It's been given to you to Glorify YOUR God! John 3:16-17

And, yet another it. (Your Clothing)
  Does **it** expose?
  Does **it** reveal?
  Does **it** entice?
Do you wear **it** because THEY wear **it**?

  If your answer is yes, then His
  response is .... <u>NO!</u>

Is **it** appropriate for church?
Would you change if you were going on a job interview?
Would you change it if you were going to court?
Would you change if you were meeting the President?
Would you change if you're meeting your future in-laws?
If your answer is yes, then His response is .... NO!

Is your bounce higher than your praise?
Is your shape more noticeable than your character?
If your neighbors didn't see your Bible,
     would they think you are going to a party?
If your answer is yes, then His response is .... NO!
If you stood in a "line-up",
     would a person pick YOU as the Christian?
BUT,
It is mine... I paid my money for **it**.
  The answer is:
Yes, but **it's** supposed to glorify YOUR God! I Peter 3:3-4

Now, just one more it. (Your Sexuality)
Must you flaunt **it**?
I won't fit-in.......... if I don't!
I won't get dates.... if I don't!

They'll think I'm stuck-up ....if I don't!
They'll laugh behind my back .....if I don't!
If you must lower your standards, to fit in, what does that say
about your friendships?

Why do you feel pressured to do **it** even though you know **it** is wrong outside of marriage?

Is **it** *really* wrong?   God says, wait.
But what if we are truly in love?   God says, wait.
But we're going to get married anyway
                                                    God says, Wait!
They especially NEED **it**.
If I won't, they'll find someone who will. God says, Wait!
I NEED **it**!
If they won't, I'll find someone who will. God says, Wait!
We will do **it** *safely*:
I promise to use protection.   God says, Wait!
I will only do **it** meaningfully
(no one-night stands)   God says, Wait!
I'll ask my partner if they're *clean* of STDs
                                          God says NO!!! Wait!!
My partner will PROVE they're clean of STDs
                                          God still says— Wait!!

If we get pregnant,
Will God still love us?   Yes
Will God love our baby?   Yes
Then what's the problem?

It is mine and God gave **it** to me!!
    The answer is:
It's been given to you to GLORIFY your God! I Cor 6:18-20

But what if it is too late.
I am no longer a virgin anyway.
I may as well keep on doing **it**.
Once you have started, you can't just stop.
The answer is:
In Christ, you are a new creature, old things are passed away.
    Behold, ALL things are become new
It's been given to you, <u>again</u>, to GLORIFY YOUR GOD!
                                                    II Cor. 5:17

Do You Still Believe in Santa?

2007

As a youngster, I was a real tomboy. I did not like sports like a lot of tomboys; but, man, I did get into mischief. I was always under stuff (like porches, houses with crawl spaces, gutter systems, etc.) or over stuff (like rooftops, up a tree, or climbing telephone poles). My girlfriends and I had a band; Robin Hood was big in my day. Today it would be called a gang; however, we did not have the negative side. We were just a bunch of girls that played outside together. It was a more innocent age. Most of the band turned increasingly *girly* as we hit the junior high school years. I changed too, but I was a lot less graceful than my friends. When they were watching *Gidget,* wearing eye shadow, and learning to

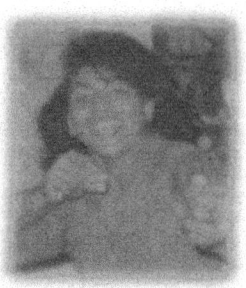

walk in pumps, I was more of the opinion that E*lly May Clampett* was my kind of girl and ponytails were as dressy as I ever needed to be. It was about this time when I found out there was no Santa Claus.

I was probably older than most kids when it sunk in. I had a real system of hope in my belief in Santa. I had rationalized the whole thing. I believed in Jesus; He was the one that told Santa who was truly good or not. Jesus was God. He handled my soul and the stuff when I died. But Santa, he was the one that handled the TOYS. He would save me from the sea of Barbie dolls, bows, and Easy-Bake Ovens that kept popping up at birthdays and Christmas. In this way, as I was asking my questions about Santa, I was really asking (unknown to the people questioned) if there was any hope that someone would ever buy me the firetruck I wanted or some tools. Would I ever get my own pair of combat boots, a baseball cap, or dare I dream of the Swiss Army knife set I had seen in the catalogs.

I wanted the dolls too; they could ride on the trucks.
Easy-Bake Ovens can be taken apart and reassembled....
if only you have a tool set.
They could keep the bows.

I came to realize in my twenties that in the homophobic age of the '50s and '60s, there was no way my mother and father would have bought their daughter those types of toys. I probably knew it then. Maybe not the why; but it was obvious my parents were not in tune with the fact that my hope chest was more like a toolbox.

For whatever reason, people associate the talents that a child displays with their sexuality. The girl, like me with the gift of crafts, is expected to limit her creative hands to scissors, glitter, and glue. God forbid she get under the sink and fix the plumbing or want to design furniture. Even though you may be open-minded enough for that, what about the budding clothes designer. The little boy that likes dressing Barbie dolls. What does that have to do with his sexuality? Outside of the fact that most of the men, around him, will keep drilling into his head that "only girls like baby dolls" he may never have felt a sexual connection. Then there is the teasing of his peers that confirm the paranoid comments of the adults. The kid does not stand a chance unless God swoops him up, into His bosom, and assures him of his worthiness. I believe, the self-image we encourage, or not, has much more to do with a child's budding sexuality than which toys they play with.

That was why Santa was so important to me. I knew everybody loved me, but the hope of being understood rested in my hope of Santa. Santa was my hope that one day, despite the nebulous condition of *being good*, I would get what I genuinely wanted; there was still hope.

I had reasoned, years earlier that "no white man ever came in my neighborhood givin' out free stuff." This caused me to start asking questions. I mean, after all, you are asking me not to climb, dig, crawl, bounce, hit, kick, scream, scrawk, or whistle. I had to give up my beloved Mumbley Peg and a host of other fun stuff too. You know, be *good*.

> Mumbley Peg, as we knew it, was a game played with a knife. We used a screwdriver since we were too young to play with knives. After all, that was our definition of lady-like, "Ladies don't play with knives." We took turns throwing from increasingly difficult places and positions, like touching the screwdriver point to the top of your head and flipping it downward, into the dirt, as you twisted into a weird position like a contortionist, trying to have it land blade down, standing on its own, in the dirt. To add difficulty, we threw into a circle drawn in the dirt. The size of the circle separated the "chimps from the chumps".

> That was why we played under porches and under houses. First, the ground was the right texture there and second our moms would have "skinned us alive" if they knew what we were playing.

I was never surprised, as Christmases went by, when I did not receive the desires of my heart. After all, I never quite measured up to that *good girl.* But Santa never gave me coals either. Therefore, I must have been "not bad", I just had not made it to *good* jus' yet. Never did I imagine that he did not exist. Even when I found the toys hidden in the closet, Daddy said, "Santa made an early delivery." I asked my mother and father, but their answers were not enough. I reasoned in my childish mind, *this was too important a decision, and Momma and Daddy did not know anything they were talking about. They didn't even know as much as I did about most things!*

I asked the other adult "authorities" (teachers, neighbors, aunts, uncles, people at church, and parents of friends). Surely, THEY knew. Then, I asked my older sisters; I called them stupid, but if the truth be told, they did know some surprisingly good stuff. I even asked the mailman; I asked him for Santa's address. Surely, if the mailman had an address—

Everybody told me it was safe. They probably were in fact giving the normal adult answers: "Santa is who you think he is", "Santa comes for all the good boys and girls", or "You are never too old to believe in Santa". But to me, clinging to my hope of being understood, I was hearing "TRUST me, there is a Santa." So, I trusted beyond my reasoning, beyond what I could see before my face. I trusted those above me. Those, I had been taught, were there to guide me—a blind trust. Consequently, when I found that there was no Santa, I felt totally betrayed. I was ENRAGED! Not only had my hopes been dashed, I additionally had been the butt of a cruel joke—I *sucked it up*, eventually, and moved on (so I thought).

The adventures of my childhood proved quite useful as I grew older. During my years as a housewife, my gift of crafts especially manifested. Once, I found myself in the crawl space under an elderly neighbor's house fixing her plumbing. Her husband had recently passed, and she received a gigantic water bill. The spiders bothered me more than they had when I was a young girl; nevertheless, being in the crawl space brought back the memories of playing Mumbley Peg.

The electric screwdriver my husband (and sons) bought me one Mother's Day is probably my most cherished gift, even now, probably twenty years after receiving it, though its engine burned out years ago. It lies in the bottom of my toolbox; yes, I eventually brought myself that toolbox. The boys and I used it many times for projects ranging from building dog houses to hanging ceiling fans.

This past Mother's Day my middle son, Kienen, presented me with an interestingly handy tool; I just loved it. He told me that his friends thought he was crazy when he said he was heading to Home Depot to get a Mother's Day present. He replied to them, "You don't know my mamma!"

I recently remembered the feelings I thought were buried long ago. I never understood why certain circumstances would make me so very angry until the following subconscious excitation bubbled that old anger to the surface like a geyser.

I was at work, sitting at my desk, looking around the office at the other people and their workstations. Though I had often referred to myself as the bottom of the totem pole, this was the moment I realized, with great disappointment, that there was indeed a glass ceiling that kept me lower than my coworkers. I had been trying to get management to realize that they were not being fair. Our positions were supposed to be equal, but training and assignments were not. Suggestions were not received equally. Responsibility was not levied equally.

Whenever I complained, I was told, "Oh, no... You ARE highly qualified!" When I asked for more, I was ignored. When I said I was not being treated with equal respect, I was called thin-skinned. When I spoke up because my turn was skipped, I was said to have an anger problem. I needed to find my groove; again, that undefined *good girl*.

Finally, I saw that the next rung on my career-ladder was just a hologram. My co-workers were already standing on their next rung; some were getting ready to climb even higher. I screamed inside my head, "*I have never felt such betrayal—not since I found out there was no Santa Claus!*" It took a few days to come to a true understanding of that gut-level exclamation.

> For years, I trusted those in authority: my supervisor, the directors, and human resource personnel. I trusted beyond what I saw, beyond the feelings of unfair treatment. Though I documented all that I thought to be unfair, I still had hope that SOMEONE would see me for who THEY said I am—"Highly Qualified"!

Then I saw the joke and, again, seemingly I was the butt of it.

> Yes, I was enraged. But this time it caused growth. I looked back at the many moments of great anger in my life and saw that I had trusted in people too blindly. However, God had used those experiences to reveal Himself to me and teach me to trust HIM.

Now, I truly have Jesus! He is no longer ruler over the "dead people's stuff". He is ruler over my LIFE. I do not need to ask the mailman for His address. I do not need the neighbors to clarify. He understands and rectifies; I don't need to ask if He exists. I KNOW HE IS!

> As it pertains to my career, like David against Goliath, I WILL STAND! I stand because you call my God a liar when you set out to constrain me.

Again, God calls me to stand.
This time He did not say *stand still*. He says:

> *STAND! Stand FOR me! You can trust ME!*

> *That is what I've been telling you all this time.*
> *TRUST Me! I know you—STAND!*

Matthew 10:30-33

Dig/Dug

2008

If I dig a <u>useless</u> hole, it may seem good exercise.

If I dig a <u>useless</u> hole for hours and hours every day,
    my time spent there seems worthless
    though it may have been good exercise.

If I dig a <u>useless</u> hole and I turn away employment,
    my digging seems foolish
    even though it may be good exercise.

If I buy new and powerful tools to dig a <u>useless</u> hole,
    my digging seems financially irresponsible
    and I didn't even get any exercise.—

If I dig a <u>useless</u> hole beyond all hopes of the hole ever
having comparative value to the time and cost of digging,
    I seem to dig in vain.
If I'm proud of my <u>useless</u> hole and the life spent digging it,
    I seem to have made a career of nonsense.

If they bury me in my ~~useless~~ hole,
    I have given purpose to my life's work.

If others read my epitaph <u>and live</u> because of it,
    God be Glorified!!

A Journey Onward:

I have been traveling quite a while, yet the journey itself has been significant. The Israelites journeyed forty years. Not because it was needed; the trip could have been made in a matter of months. It only took that long because of their stiff necks.

I am not sure what lies ahead, but I will move when Jesus leads:

> *I do not know how long 'twill be*
> *Nor what the future holds for me*
> *But this I know,*
> *If Jesus leads me,*
> *I shall get home someday.*
>
> Tindley 1916

2009

God has paused the journal. I have nothing new to write. Yet, He has made it clear that this is not the end. Therefore, all of 2009 has been spent editing. That isn't a bad thing because reading and re-reading these stories have reminded me of the many lessons God taught me and has driven an awakening, unto Him, deep into my every thought.

Life, cycles.

Never in my wildest dreams would I have imagined the hills and valleys a lifetime would bring. God strengthens us, on the hillsides, in preparation for the valleys. However, He doesn't leave us to travel alone. In the valley, He is the friend who walks quietly along, waiting for us to speak first.

Over 30 years ago   There was a knock at my front door; it was a salesman. What was he selling? Grave sites! I thought it was something weird to be selling door-to-door, but what the hey! It was a safer time when you actually let people in your house that you did not know, listened to their spiel, and sometimes even bought what they were selling. He had a hard-sell presentation and talked as if he were selling real estate; neither of which sold me. To keep my interest, he had to switch his sales tactics. I did not want to think about being underground; thoughts about water and worms were too creepy. I think he sensed it because he switched from graves to mausoleums.

It may seem trivial, but I know me. The hard sell would usually do nothing but make me dig my heels in and refuse to buy *anything* just to prove my will was stronger than their sales pitch. Other than the fact that I am the child of an accountant, I may not have understood the terms he used like "Estate

Planning", "Real Property", and "Prepaid"; not back then anyway. Truthfully, I am surprised he even kept my attention long enough to make the sale. In fact, I used to think those terms were the ONLY reasons he made the sale. In hindsight, it was undeniably wise financially.

The whole time the salesman was talking I was trying to keep my rambunctious two-year-old son, Timothy, under control. I decided that if/when something should happen to me, he would not have to buy it. It was only $12 a month (for what seemed forever), but I was committed, to my son, to pay the whole amount.

I ended up picking a slot inside the building just in case my funeral was during bad weather; I thought that would be easier on the guests. I picked a slot on the next-to-the-top row because I figured the top was too high and I did not want to pick a slot on either of the bottom two rows after growing up sleeping in bunk beds. I was twenty-two years old and did not think much deeper than that.

The location of the cemetery intimidated me; it was across town from where I lived. It was in a much more affluent neighborhood but, that did not impress me. I figured I would not know about it when I used it. I was always afraid to go see the mausoleum because I was petrified about getting lost.

During my grace period, I did my due diligence and checked out the company and the cemetery by calling the numbers on the contract and checking the Better Business Bureau. I even called the cemeteries in my area and asked about this one. Later, when the internet got more popular, I looked up the website and got more information; however, I never went to see it. I knew it was truly there and that was enough for me. I always told myself that when the time came, the hearse would drive me and anybody else, wanting to go, could follow.

As the years went on and times got hard, I sometimes fell behind in the payments. I even renegotiated the payments down to $8 a month, but like I said, I was committed to paying the whole price. It became a real obsession of mine to pay this thing off. I refused to lose the money I had spent. If I did not need it, I could sell it. The salesman had said something about it building equity.

> I knew that the company did not expect me to finish and had probably planned it that way. For every person who neglected to make payments, they could pocket all the money from the day of sale to the day of default, with no exchange of product. All they had to do was close the account and sell it again, probably at a higher price because of inflation. That was why I was so determined. I wanted to beat their odds! And, whether I used it or built equity, it was something I could do at age twenty-two, to work towards my son's future.

After many years, I set the payments on an automatic payment from my bank account; I never thought about it again, except the few times when we did other things having to do with estate planning like changing life insurance and configuring my LLC and trust. Life went on…

Over Five Years Ago   My mother, being an accountant and getting up in age, started asking my sisters and me to hold family meetings in an effort to make sure that my father, all my siblings, and I knew the details of our family finances, caretaking arrangements, death benefits, and memorial preparations. At first, none of us wanted to hear it. One day she invited us to the *Cheesecake Factory* for dinner. None of us knew her plan, but right after we all ordered our meals, she reached down into some case we had not noticed and pulled out folders with everyone's names on them. She very nicely, as if she was in a board meeting, passed them out and started to explain each paper to us. When dinner started to come, she collected the folders and continued to talk while we ate. We finally realized why we needed to know all that *stuff* and called an actual meeting soon thereafter.

Those meetings made me realize that my finances needed some objective organization. Though I was handling my finances well, all the details were in my head. The ramifications of any major illness or catastrophe would be amplified because of my sons' lack of knowledge and inability to gain access to my accounts. So, I set out to make the necessary changes.

After updating my documentation, I started talking to my eldest son, Timothy, about my final wishes. No absolute, formal discussions, just mentioning things in general conversation. It was a natural flow since we worked together every Sunday.

I mentioned one of these conversations in a previous story when I wrote about Timothy and Kienen helping me trim the trees. I mentioned us laughing about their promise to cut the trees down no LESS than two weeks after my death. During that conversation we most likely talked about more than just trees. I usually used such opportunities to slip in other tidbits of information about final arrangements as well.

Several times Tim and I had conversations about cremation; the pros and cons. I don't remember exactly how the subject kept coming up; but it did. I do know that once he realized that I wanted to be cremated, he kept trying to convince me otherwise. I finally conceded. For whatever reason Tim was adamant about cremation and would not have peace if I was cremated. So, I thought to let him have his way, even though it did not make sense to me.

Because of those conversations, Tim and I got into some remarkably deep discussions about our preferences in life-and-death decisions, arrangements, displays, etc. We talked about all kinds of topics that most people don't usually think to talk about. He was very interested in what I wanted and liked. He thought it would make a difficult time easier if anything happened to me. I KNEW, in a way, these talks were helping all my sons. Tim NEEDED to know! He would be totally overwhelmed if he didn't. If I died and left Timothy clueless, that would be a catastrophe on so many levels! So, we often laughed our way through a lot of information that would have otherwise been too much for him to process. He knew my choice in caskets, my favorite flowers, my choice in clothing, and my music preferences. I even wrote my own eulogy. He knew about the mausoleum and the payments. He also knew about my notes and where all my keys and codes were.

One thing about this type of sharing was that it wasn't just about giving him a list. In exchanging information through conversation, Tim got to know ME, and I think that was more important to him. On the other hand though, I got to KNOW him too. I knew his favorite colors, his music, his flowers, his favorite suit, his love of his cowboy boots, which hats he liked best, how he washed his dreadlocks—why he did what he did the way he did it. I knew his favorite candy, his favorite food. I got to know the kind of woman he wanted to marry and why. I got to know what he loved about children. I knew his love for animals and why he did so well with them. I sincerely got to know HIM.

Three Years Ago   Last night, I had the most frightening dream. In it, I stood at the top of a cliff watching down into a valley of winding roads. As I watched, there were several cars driving up the hill. Suddenly, I saw one of the cars heading into a horrific accident. From my vantage point, I watched what was going to happen, and then, in Technicolor slow motion, what DID happen. While realizing that I was helpless to warn the driver, I recognized it was *my son's* car. I woke suddenly in a panic.

> The car in the dream did not actually belong to either of my boys. But the emotion of watching what was, symbolically, one of my sons end up in a horrific accident was a warning that shook me to my core. I awoke with the need to immediately make sure I got closer to each of them by saying the things I always forgot to say, warning them of the things I was too shy to discuss and talking about their relationships, earthly and heavenly. Basically, getting in their business even though—as Tim would say—they were GROWN men!

So, the conversations that, in the past, were between Tim and me were now discussions with all three of them and a little more pointed into THEIR lives.

Two Years Ago   After working more than ten years together, Tim and I had a dreadful argument that split us up. He decided he did not want to work for the LLC any longer; this was good because I was avoiding the idea of firing my own son. You see, where all the conversations I spoke of earlier were genuinely pleasant and we did have a lot of good hearty laughs together; additionally, we had difficult times. Though I was grooming him to take over in a few years, there were times when Tim did not want to follow direction; he wanted autonomy NOW! So, as the climax of many dramatic moments, Timothy refused to do *it* the way I wanted *it* done, he decided to *walk off the job*. I concluded that since he wanted to walk off the job, I would let him walk home besides. In truth, I dropped him at a bus stop; he was the one who chose to walk the four to five miles instead of catching the bus. Suffice it to say he was angry with me. I guess I was supposed to back down and drive him home—I did not; I knew he had money and had other options (i.e., bus or cab). At least I did not make him carry his tools. I drove them over later.

That happened sometime in August, maybe early September. By Thanksgiving he was still not speaking. Thanksgiving being his favorite holiday, he cut off his own nose to spite his face and refused to join the family for dinner at my parent's house.

> After so many years of working together, this was an extremely difficult time for me. Not so much that he was angry (I felt I was right), but I missed his presence.

> In May 2008, I left my full-time position of over twenty-five years with the Federal Government in an EEO[35] settlement.[36] Since then, Timothy and I were working together fulltime which meant we spoke, on the phone, almost every morning to plan the day's activity. It was these early morning phone calls that I missed so much.

It was no surprise when he did not call during the Christmas season because that was his least favorite holiday; it was his custom to withdraw from all the *fa-la-la hoopla*. In January, I spoke to him on his birthday; however, it was a labored conversation. He accepted my reaching out to him, but he had trouble reaching back to me because, in his mind, that counted as an apology.

When Valentine's Day rolled around, and he was still keeping his distance, I recognized that he had dug himself into a deep hole, and his ego would not let him come out. I figured he

---

[35] Equal Employment Opportunity

[36] Referencing back to the story *Do You Still Believe in Santa*: I told you I didn't need Santa Claus. God told me to STAND, and he took care of the rest. Despite my fears and distress, God stood up and showed out!

missed my presence just as much as I missed his. SO, instead of doing my regular thing and buying a gag gift for Valentines' Day, I bought Timothy a box of chocolate caramels (his favorite) and a card. I don't remember what it said, except it was a funny card that said something like *you may be mad, but I bet you'll eat my candy.* I don't remember the conversation that ensued; nonetheless, I know one did. I don't even remember calling him a few days later and asking him to help me with a tree that fell during the big snowstorm, but I know I did. How do I know? Because I remember looking out my back window 370 days ago and realizing the tree was cut down and laid in the back corner of the yard, where the garden used to be. I remember thinking that Tim probably planned to cut it into smaller pieces when the weather broke.

370 days ago
February 23, 2010

8:00 a.m.: The electrician called and said that there was no one at the property to let him in. I started calling Tim and got no answer. This was odd; Tim was NEVER late meeting service people because he knew they would charge me just for coming out. Did he oversleep? I kept calling...

10:00 a.m.: He still isn't answering. Now, I was angry. I remember wondering, *Has he gotten an attitude about something?* That was when I noticed the tree in the backyard. He had to have cut it down yesterday; I was out there yesterday morning, and it hadn't been done yet. I knew he was over any anger because the tree was so nicely cut and laid in the corner. Otherwise, he would have chopped it down and thrown it in the middle of the yard. I know my son..."

11:00 a.m.: I was worried. My thoughts were racing, *Where is Tim? Why isn't he answering my calls? There is NO reason he would not have called me by now, especially if he remembered the service call this morning. Did he forget? But we just spoke about it! Maybe his phone is dead... I'll text everyone that may have ANY idea where Tim could be.*

11:30 a.m.

... 12:00 noon

Momma's Lullaby

Timmy sleeps…
Rock my baby and put him to bed.

No more struggles …
Rock my baby and put him to bed.

What flowers to pick?
Roses? … 'Twernt nothin' rosey 'bout Timmy but the thorns.
Timmy's my Wild-Flower Child; my child of the field.
Rained on; Snowed on; Left standin' lone in the heat of the day.
Rock my baby and put him to bed.

What clothes to pick?
Suit? Dashiki? Jeans? Motorcycle Helmet?
It don't matter, he's asleep. Leave 'em with his boots off.
Rock my baby and put him to bed.

What music? … Only His music!
What picture?
Timmy don't like no pictures…
REMEMBER the good times!
Rock my baby and put him to bed.

Does Timmy know Jesus?
He wrote a song about Him—
Here how it go…
Rock my baby and put him to bed.

Timmy sleeps now…
Rock a while…
Rock my baby and put him to bed.

By God's grace, see him in the mornin'.
Rock my baby and put him to bed.

For the last 300 days or so   When people gave condolences, I could smile. I knew God had it all covered. I closed Tim's accounts and handled his affairs. I learned how bad things were. With all the "Past Due" notices, rejection letters, and closing accounts, I saw that the bottom was just about to collapse around him. I thought it merciful that God did not make him suffer with, what I saw to be, the impossibilities getting ready to engulf him. From the nature of the notices, I believe Tim never knew. I told many people that it was God's grace and mercy that allowed Tim to sleep, and I meant it.

Five days ago   God said, *Hold-up baby girl! You have it ALL twisted! I did not set the timing according to the situation. I set the situation according to the timing!*

What?

About a month after his death, Tim's *lifelines* were gone. His money, his relationships, most of his worldly commitments—all the glue, that held his life together, dissipated, and like a hand removed from sand, it all came crashing in within a month or so. I saw the trend develop and end so quickly that it startled me. Yes, for the last three hundred days or so, I have been thinking the bottom was getting ready to fall out for Tim and counted him blessed. But, just now, God corrected me. God showed me that HE had ended Tim's *lifelines* because they were no longer needed. It was HIS hand that was removed from the sand.

Wow! Oh My GOD! God sustained Tim his ENTIRE life! Like two congruent lines, Tim's destiny and God's care travelled together Timothy's WHOLE life's span. Sometimes the lines drew close, even touched. Through all of Tim's travels, God's care sustained him. When Tim veered this way or that, God's care was always there. When Tim's life ended, God's earthly care ended. Timothy no longer needed it. If he had needed it any longer, God would have sustained him longer.

Because I don't talk about the circumstances of Timothy's death, I think some people assume I am ashamed of him somehow. Quite the contrary, like I've said many times, my goal was to raise men not boys and that's what I did. I raised three *Big Dogs* [37]—of totally different breeds (personalities); but each stand firm with good hearts and strong characters. I am proud of them ALL!

I don't know the details of Tim's death. I DO know he died while helping a friend even though he was left alone in the battle. It still bothers me that I don't know Tim's last words. I believe he died in pain and fear. I hope he remembered to call on Jesus—his TRUE friend and provider.

Today   Timothy lies asleep[38], waiting for the Lord's return[39], in the mausoleum bought years ago while he ran around the room ducking and dodging under the tables and chairs. I'm so glad I chose something aboveground; each rainstorm would be traumatic for me. I am glad I picked indoors; the bad weather did not cause problems during his funeral or when I've gone to dress his grave. Being next to the top row makes everyone look up to him; he would like that. I still have the fear of getting lost when I go, but now I can use my GPS.

We did not need to find the $20,000 (today's cost) to purchase the crypt because the *prepaid* account was almost paid off. If I had kept paying $12 monthly, instead of $8, I believe it would have been paid. The lady at the cemetery said how she admired my planning at such a young age. It wasn't me—nothing but God! I see His hands all over it! I knew the flowers, I knew the music, I knew which suit, and I knew exactly what Timothy would have wanted. We had had many conversations, laughing

---

[37] From *All Men are Dogs* – if you haven't read the story, this probably doesn't mean what you think!

[38] John 11:11-14

[39] I Thessalonians 4:16

through ideas that would have been way too overwhelming for ME to process.

Many people grieve the last argument, not I. At the time, I thought it was so very difficult every morning when I wanted to hear Tim say, "Hey Ma, what's up?" It was God's grace that allowed me six months to adjust while I thought Tim was just being stubborn; the silence would have haunted me otherwise. Tim's physical absence, during those months was another instance of God's mercy. God let me learn how to run the business, and even exist, without Tim's help. Just as I always say—God NEVER lets me walk blindly into a situation; He ALWAYS prepares me for the situation or prepares the situation for me. I Kings 17:8-10

> God was so very thorough that He did not even let it end with the argument. What I saw as a struggle against Timothy's frustrating stubbornness was in reality the angels pushing us apart preparing us BOTH for what was to come. Tim had to learn, QUICKLY, to lean solely on God, not Mom. I had to learn just as quickly to find the other people I needed to help do all the things Tim used to handle. Psalm 23:4-5

Even in the midst of that separation, God shook me and told me "Not a gag gift this time. Give Timothy something sweet." Because of that, I know that Tim was aware I loved him as he ate each piece of his favorite candy on Valentine's Day, nine days before his death.

Tim left a love note for me, too—the tree and its branches that he laid neatly in the corner of my yard. Psalm 23:6 SELAH

> With every memory of Timothy, there is almost always a lesson associated. Reflecting on an example of his *climbing the rough side of the mountain,* I remember, when he was about twelve years old, that there was an extremely steep hill near our home. I had given strict

instructions, to all three boys, that they were NEVER to try riding their bikes down that hill. When DRIVING down that hill in a car, you literally looked down over your hood and saw a view resembling a roller coaster ride. Of course, Tim had to try it; I knew what he had done the minute I saw him limping down the street, carrying his bent front wheel over one shoulder. He was pushing the frame with one hand; and, guiding it with the other, as the remaining wheel wobbled profusely.

He looked pitiful with all the bruises and scrapes, some of which never went away. I did not fuss. All I said was "Tim, I know you heard a small voice telling you to stop. Please, listen to Him next time." Timothy looked surprised and said, "How did you know?" I told him that I knew MY God would not let someone (that I loved) do such a silly thing without saying something.

In his adult years, Timothy was continually searching for God, and just as sure as I knew God spoke to him at the top of that hill when he was a boy, I also know God did not let Timothy's search go unanswered. I can rest assured that God indeed revealed Himself to Tim. Maybe death was God's way to keep him from losing the relationship for which he had searched so long.

Whatever the reason, when I see God's handwriting all over the script, like I see it here, there are NO questions to ask—only one response: Amen, AMEN and again AMEN!

What a mighty God we serve!

Through the
Valley of the Shadow of Death
"Understanding the *Closet Down the Hall*"

2012

The graduation celebration went well, and I was able to hold it together; however, inside, I was a basket case. I missed Timothy immensely. Tim and I were hangout buddies when it came to occasions like this; he would NEVER have missed his brother's graduation. Supporting his brothers was a very big deal to him, so sitting there without him bought waves of mourning. Waves because mixed with the mourning was celebration of my son's big day.

I was filled with joy that David, my baby boy, was graduating from college with a degree in Information Technology—the

very subject he had hated as a youngster. In reality, he was quite the man. He'd been in the military and was married with kids. But, to me, he'll always be *MY baby boy*!

I sat there remembering the period when David was angry with me for leaving to go to work, calling me a *work-o-holic*. He had a hard time adjusting to my transition from a homeschooling, stay-at-home mom re-entering the workforce as a computer specialist. David rejected everything I taught them about computers until he reached High School. That is when he and his older brother, Kienen, were living in boarding school and found that there was a need for computer repairmen around campus. The need sparked the entrepreneurial spirit in which they had been raised, and the ongoing joke became: *Oh, the wonders of duct tape*!

> They had components stacked all over their perspective living quarters where they built, repaired, and refurbished *Frankenstein-ed* computers for friends and classmates. So, I was extremely proud to see him walk the stage.

It was a rollercoaster of emotion. One minute I was elated and the next minute deeply depressed that Tim wasn't there with us.

I was trying my best NOT to be a wet blanket. So, I hid my mourning and waited until everything was over. I quoted Tim a couple of times, but I didn't talk about how he would have wanted to be there, etc. When everyone left to go their separate ways, I took a trip to the mausoleum and walked the surrounding cemetery. I walked while reading gravestones and noting the life spans depicted by the dates on grave markers. I looked at the dates and correlated them with world events. Occasionally I do that; it helps me feel connected to the others that mourn and reminds me that it isn't just me. That usually *stopped the burning*.

> Like being burned by hot grease; you first stop the burning effect of the grease, then you address the healing of the wound.

When I left the cemetery, I went to Home Depot to purchase some padlocks. When I arrived, the emotional pain was almost unbearable.

> Anyone that has put their arm in a hot oven, with a not yet healed burn wound, knows the intense pain you get from the sensitive skin. Any other time the temperature of the oven would not bother you. It is just that the wounded area is still so sensitive—

> that was what it felt like in Home Depot.

For over ten years, Tim and I had spent every Sunday morning in Home Depot getting supplies for the day/week. The first time I went there after his death was horrific, but I forced myself through it. That was a little over a year ago. It got easier as time went by. Now, I seldom get depressed. I always think of Tim, because we brainstormed so much, but seldom does it cause pain anymore. Usually I try to think, *What would Timmy say?* And that usually helps me think my way through a problem.

> Tim hated to ask the men there for help. He did, however, get a kick out of watching me *play* the helpless woman. So, when I need to ask for help now, it brings a tickle to my heart remembering Tim mimicking me by saying in a sing-y voice, *"Oh sir, what-so-ever-shall-I-dooo?"*.

Tonight, I could tell my face was showing my pain. I saw it in the looks of the attendants that were helping me. I just sucked it up and refused to give in to the wave of sorrow that was trying to engulf me.

> Now, I understand the pain of a person in grief. Where, before Tim's death, I couldn't understand why people couldn't just move on. Now, I realize it is like losing a limb; you must first heal and then you can start to learn to live without them. For some, including myself, recovery may be a whole different phase than learning to move on.

A year after Tim's death, I essentially felt my mind snap back into place. Though I had been going through the motions, I didn't realize that I was not functioning completely up to speed. I thought I was fine and doing quite well. Only in hindsight do I recognize the big mistakes I made with some contracts and commitments.

I have NO idea what the technique is called and did not purposely use it as my way of coping. But now, I realize that I locked all my deep, dark emotions about Tim's death in a *closet at the end of the hall*. It was an emotional closet that I built years ago to store all my unproductive emotions. All those emotions that did nothing but get me into trouble.

In the past, my emotional baggage was just thrown into the closet and the door was shut. If I wanted to drudge up something, the thought of digging through all the "stuff" was usually enough to make me drop the subject. However, with Timothy's death, the emotions had REAL life. It was like forcing a gorilla into the closet. I even had to put a padlock on the door to keep it shut. Sometimes, like today, I hear pounding, from *the closet*, even though I'm downstairs in the *living room*.

This technique does generally work. So far, it has made it possible for me to constrain *the gorilla* and remain functional; but woe to people that venture down that hallway.

In actuality, if you get to the closet, you have crossed so many boundaries and are so deep into my personal space that if you venture even further and *pick the lock* and *open the door,* you DESERVE the gorilla you will face!

You may think I need to deal with that gorilla. Nope, I refuse! Another person brought that gorilla and dumped him on me. I feel that I give him more power by giving him attention. I've given his existence to God to handle.

Caution:

He who seeks skeletons may fine gorilla instead…

GAP - (Gospel According to Pam!)

Be Fruitful and Multiply

May **2013**

and—I'm not talking about in Genesis[40]

- If your dream isn't growing, check your SOIL
- Recognize the sidewalk:
  - Don't waste seed
  - Sow the FIELD not the sidewalk
- Worldly wisdom can't understand Godly growth.

Eternal Life INCLUDES Today![41]

The FIFTH Season   2014

(Pastor JL McLellan – my eldest sister)

Spring, Summer, Fall, Winter—and *Due Season* [42]
Don't tire of doing the right thing, just because it's right!
the day of the righteous is coming!

---

[40] Matthew 13:23
[41] Job 42:12-13
[42] Leviticus 26:3-4; Luke 12: 42-44; Galatians 6:9

Forward into Freedom 2014

- *w/o comfort in complacency*
- *w/o paralysis of analysis*
- *w/o procrastination*
- *w/o fear*

I'm dreaming of moving to a small ranch in Colorado. However, I realize that that dream was a plan made with Timothy. Do I still honestly want to move into such isolation at my age? Yes, I love being around me!

I took the trip; I flew to Kansas and drove to and from Las Vegas through Colorado, driving more than fifty hours all over Colorado. The most BEAUTIFUL country I have ever seen! It was a WONDERFUL road trip—just me, my GPS, and I— stopping to talk with the "locals" all along the way.

I learned several things that "Maps" and Google couldn't relay; the MOST important being what living *downwind* of a working livestock ranch means. Also, as important, the differing of minds in Colorado vs Utah.

I thoroughly enjoyed the adventure, totally out of my comfort zone. I never knew I enjoyed driving so much! Around mountain landscapes, down long dirt roads, along winding streams, even past bucks in ditches so deep that only the tips of their antlers showed. Sometimes I had to get out of the car and just LOOK!

I would love the adventure of moving on top of a hill in nowhere! But I can't be such a burden to my sons. I need to be realistic since I am getting older now. So, it becomes a dream released.

Maybe the thought of moving to Colorado was just enough to make me do something I never would have done otherwise; driving fifty hours with only a GPS; this trip was AMAZING!

Color to the edge of the Page
(It reduces the *MARGIN* of ERROR)

September **2016**

In children's coloring books, there are usually bold black lines that "define" the outer edge of pictures to be colored. We teach our children to "stay inside the lines" for nice, neat pictures.

As adults, *staying in the lines* has usually become second nature and tends to instinctually drive us to stay within our assigned area of operation. When two divisions work together as a team, we tend to expect each of them to *color up to their side of the bold line* and STOP!

> My group had completed our portion of the project and stopped at the *line*, as told. We wanted an excellent presentation and checked with our counterparts several times. They insisted that they had plenty of time and everything was under control. When it was time for the presentation, my group was left with a mediocre presentation because of missing details the others had not completed.

> God spoke straight into my heart, *From now on, color to the edge of the page.* I knew exactly what He meant.

> It doesn't take much, just persistence. The *border* people SHOULD be given ample time to *color*; however, when it gets down to the wire and the *borders* are not done, don't just stand and wait. No matter how well the *picture* is colored, the fine framing points of *the border* can make or break the total effect.

Keeping the *big picture* in mind: though the *border* completed by the BORDER Division may have been best; through God's grace, the *border* completed by the PICTURE Division can similarly be executed in excellence, if needed. I Cor 10:31

Ant Attack

2017

Have you ever lived through an ant attack? I've lived through several. Not because I have a dirty house, but because I don't like to use a lot of chemicals. There is ONE main rule to ending the attack QUICKLY:

Don't focus on killing the ants!

- Find the *Attraction* and remove it.
- Put a *Defense* in place.
- Help THEM decide to quit.
- Ants keep searching.
- They WILL find something else and another way in.
- So, be proactive.

Note: All *ants* aren't insects!

Find the ROOT of a problem and handle it.
Afterwards, the SYMPTOMS often solve themselves.

GAP-(Gospel According to Pam!)

The Little Engine that Could

Late 2017

I thought I was coping extremely well. I didn't even see the darkness of the tunnel. It had become my *new normal.* One day I looked up and saw something bright moving toward me. I watched it a while and suddenly realized it was light— light from the other end of a tunnel that I didn't even realize I was in.

Timothy is not forgotten, but I've learned to *move on.*

California here I come

It was a SNOWY day about four years ago when my middle son, Kienen, announced, "I'm out of here! I can't stand it ANYmore!" If I remember correctly, by spring, he was well into his plan to move to California— no more snow for him! He chose San Diego and has been there ever since.

I haven't been to San Diego in years; I was so excited! Having the opportunity to visit Kienen on his turf was GREAT! A mother's dream. Seeing her adult child in his home, meeting his friends, seeing his world, seeing the lessons you taught so many years ago fulfilled.

When they were younger, my mantra was *I'm not raising boys; I'm raising men!* Seeing Kienen in his element was a trip worthwhile in itself!

This was a dual purposed trip. We were, in addition, exploring the idea of me moving to the West Coast and living closer to him. The thought is quite compelling; but my grandchildren are still very young and all live on the East Coast. Maybe this will be my *Phase II* move. Phase I is going to have to be nearer to the grands—maybe some acreage in Maryland.

Here again, a trip that I may not have done otherwise. Is the Lord just sending me on vacations? That is fine! Each trip seems perfectly designed for me! An extremely relaxing adventure, with my son as my personal guide. I worried it might burden him; on the contrary he enjoyed showing off for Mom!

Following the Leader?

Dec **2018**

I drive a standard size car. Sometimes in rush hour traffic, it's just easier to get behind a big SUV that seems to be "reading the traffic" and let them guide me down the road. Occasionally, if I don't stay aware of the traffic, I'll find myself STUCK, in what I thought was a slow lane, only to find that the driver in front of me has started coasting and the traffic in front of them has, as a matter of fact, moved way down the road.

Leaders come and go. Make sure you follow ONLY they that follow Christ. Occasionally, look past your leader and make sure THEY are not the only one in front! You should always be able to see (and feel) GOD at the head of their leadership. [43]

I can't stand "driving" behind people with "tinted windows"!
GAP

---

[43] Judges 2:10

My Life's Story is My Sacrifice

Psalms 40:6-8

2019

- The word of God is written on your heart.
  You don't have to go far to find it …only within!
  Deut. 30:11-14

- When a CHOSEN people refuse to accept a calling,
  God WILL find a WILLING people.
  Luke 14:21-24

- You need oil IN your lamp; not just easy to reach.
  Matt 25:3-10

- Being forgiven is preceded by repentance.
  Luke 17:4; Acts 2:38

- My tongue should reflect the Spirit of God.
  II Sam 23:2

- The wicked conspire, but God will prevail; the day
  of the righteous is coming.
  Mal 4:1-3

- Don't work in FEAR of tomorrow, work in FAITH
  of it!
  Luke 12:30-34

- Remember God's wisdom in your old age. Don't
  let His wisdom and the many years you've
  travelled be wasted for moments of pleasure.
  I Kings 11:4

Destination-Peace

2019

Years ago, God met me at a crossroads and asked, "Which way do you want to go?" He let me know that neither road was easy. My answer was "Peace"; all I wanted to do was live in Peace. I didn't realize that residence there takes a change of mind-set, not address. Peace is the ONLY state without borders, and it does not tax its citizens.

The journey has not been easy. I have learned that Peace is not heaven. Sometimes, you are called to fight for Peace; sometimes you have to stand against the storm to reach Peace. There are mountain tops AND valleys in Peace.

I have travelled a desert full of snakes and scorpions, bitter waters, and quail. I even dealt with fierce enemies and warred with giants. But like the Israelites, God has always been there to guide me along the way.

Many years had passed since God asked me what I wanted and, inadvertently, I started just *moving with the crowd* because we seemed to be travelling in the same direction. In actuality though, I was pursuing peace and the world was chasing success. There came a point when I had to ask myself, "What is success?"

I reflected on a conversation, about success, that I had with some friends. One said, "You know you're rich when you can go to bed when you're sleepy and get up when you want." After talking about mansions, yachts, and airplanes, he continued, "When you don't have a boss prioritizing your family obligations." Another friend chimed in, saying, "It's when you have at least one dollar more than all the money you need. Then you don't have to worry to pay your bills."

Did you see it? It took me a while, but then I noticed—
I have a different definition of success. Most people
equate success with being *rich* or how much money
they have. To me, real success has nothing to do with
money or things.

> To me, success is reaching my chosen
> destination (Peace) in a sound mind, still
> connected to my source of truth (God), and
> healthy enough to enjoy the stay.

Many people choose goals like being rich, famous, even
infamous, and qualify success by the lifestyle they associate
with that goal. Their success, then, becomes measured by the
size of their house or bank account. In choosing the destination
Peace, however, there was no financial component. One can
be rich or poor in Peace. Eccles. 4:6, Prov. 15:16

I think my success was predicated by a wise choice in
destinations. How sad it would have been to travel so many
years to reach an *end point* and be unhappy.

> I absolutely adore my God-inspired DoC.
> (**D**estination **of** Choice)

I arrived a little while ago. I did not realize it, when I first
crossed Peace's boarders, but I see it now. It is similar to the
temporary quarters I visited earlier in the story *A Home in-a-
dis Kingdom*. Yet, *Peace* is more encompassing than a condo.
It is a refuge, a state (of mind), even a whole world (of
existence). Heb 11:16

> Whether or not people are kind to me,
> > I will have peace.
> Whether or not I have the ranch I once desired,
> > I will have peace.
> Whether or not I have all the money I want,
> > I will have peace.
> Whether or not others heed the call,

I will have peace.
Whether or not the lord comes tomorrow,
I will have peace.

In hindsight, I realize how often I have said that this or that did not exist in my world anymore, and I meant it. Once I have turned something over to God, I do not stress about it anymore; it is no longer in MY existence. I don't even REMEMBER to worry about it. The next time I notice whatever it is, I am usually being dumbfounded by the way God has handed it.

There is a spiritual maturity about living in *Peace.* You no longer do what YOU want and then ask God to handle your mess. Instead, you aspire to live by GOD's rules knowing he has your back if you make a mistake. Isa 26:3

Now that I realize I have arrived,
I will make *Peace* my own and call it *HOME.*
Shalom!

2020 Hindsight

Psalm 37:23

2020

None of these stories were planned. There was no outline created to develop a plot or story line. Each story or poem was scripted as I traveled through the peaks and valleys of life. It amazes me when I see that this last story, Destination Peace, answers a long-forgotten prayer that was uttered in the first story over thirty-five years prior.

It is nothing less than miraculous!

Dakota's in the House!
2020

I adopted another "Big Dog" a couple of years ago; a Blackmouth Cur/Pitt mix. Like our previous dogs, she came from a shelter. I decided to keep the name she already had— Dakota. Dakota was a beautiful puppy and is growing to be a beautiful dog! Compared to our previous dogs, Dakota is a totally different breed. (Pun intended!)

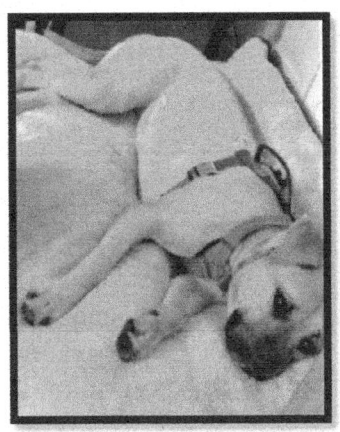

People ask me all the time,
*   "What is she?"*

- *Nikki, the dog we had when my sons were young, was a Rottweiler/Shepherd-mix that loved to follow her masters' will.*
- *Dakota, which is a Cur/Pitt-mix, challenges EVERY command. You must constantly maintain authority or, before you realize it, she will inch her way into being Pack Leader.*

Life was getting a bit mundane. I stayed in bed way too late because I had nothing to MAKE me get up. I stayed away from home because nothing MADE me come home. I was losing my drive and life was getting boring. As I stated before, Peace (here on earth anyway) sometimes needs some contrast.

Once, for a rainy-day activity with my grandchildren, we visited an animal shelter. I reminded them, before we went in, that we were there just to VISIT the animals. But there she was, the cutest mixed breed puppy I had ever seen. At the time we thought she was a Labrador mix; that is how the shelter had classified her.

She was incredibly sad and seemed to light up when we introduced ourselves. I had previously considered getting another dog; so, after some thought and three more visits, Dakota left with us for her new home.

In a sense, Dakota became my *service* animal. Being faithful to her needs and temperament kept me on my toes as her *Servant Leader*.

When I first got her home, I set alarms on my phone for her schedule for things like waking-up, feedings, nap times, and potty breaks. She has quite simple needs and she works excellently on a schedule. Her inner clock works almost to the second.

I trained her to ring a bell when she wanted to go potty or eat. Often, she rings her bell just seconds before the alarm sounds.

A little while into her training, Dakota became very difficult and did not want to follow commands. It got so bad that I almost took her back to the shelter. Then, I realized the problem. I was responding every time my cellphone sounded. In her doggy-brain, the PHONE was her *Master*. The PHONE decided when she ate, slept, and went outside; she thought the phone was in charge; she had no reason to listen to MY commands.

There is a whole lesson in the thought about us being slaves to our cellphones; but I won't go off on that tangent, right now.

To regain my *Alpha-ness,* I had to set the alarms a few minutes earlier than the event. Then, when the alarms sounded, I turned them off and continued what I was doing. A few minutes later, I would start whatever was scheduled. After a while, she understood I decided when she eats, sleeps, goes potty, etc.

As a puppy, Dakota could indeed try my patience. She was very sweet, but I had to keep our pack order absolutely defined. Even now, when she rings her bell for potty, I usually make her wait a few minutes. Otherwise, she eventually starts to ring it with authority as if to say, "Let's go NOW!"

When she races to a doorway, I make her wait; then, I go through first. If not, she finds too much pleasure in *leading* us through the door. A few times, when I forgot and unconsciously started letting her enter rooms first, she slowly slipped into being *Alpha* and started ignoring my commands again. Once, as she led us through a doorway, she looked back over her shoulder, rolled her eyes, and mumbled with a low growl.

During her first year with me, Dakota ALWAYS had *two paws on the banana peel*. If it were not for the fact that she had previously suffered a *revolving door syndrome*[44] at the shelter, I would have taken her back in a heartbeat!

As a puppy, she broke chains made for 250lbs of pressure. She went through KONG® harnesses like butter. On one occasion, before I found the right leash, she twisted my hand so badly that it took my thumb more than six months to heal. I purposely did not go to the doctor because I knew, if I were told it was broken, she WOULD be taken back.

I eventually realized her biggest problem was FEAR. Then, things turned for the better. Though she fought tooth and nail to be the *Pack Leader,* she was basically afraid of EVERYTHING! She was afraid of birds, squirrels, cats, dogs (large or small), and people; even leaves and paper bags blowing in the wind sent her into a fury.

---

[44] being given-up; adopted; given-up; and adopted

Note: Dakota did not look afraid. she LOOKED vicious! But I knew the truth.

Many of Dakota's behaviors may or may not have been a problem with other dogs; but with a dog that is extremely territorial AND fearful, I had to establish safe boundaries for her. I did this by putting dog beds in every room and putting her cage under the kitchen table. THOSE are her spots; the rest of the house is mine. She is allowed in MY areas if she abides by MY rules; otherwise, she is limited to her spots.

The only time I would allow her head to be above mine (which is a sign of dominance) was when we went up the stairs. She would race up the steps and sit there as I walked up. I climb a little slowly these days; so, she used to sit authoritatively tall as I climbed. Soon she realized that instead of being in charge she was actually WAITING. In *defiance,* she stopped sitting and waiting. Now, when she races up the steps, she casually sniffs around the area until I get up there.

However, I believe the biggest change, in her behavior, came when I boarded her, at a kennel, for ten days while I took my grandkids to Disneyland. I could tell that she was TOTALLY shocked when I returned for her. She thought she had just been abandoned at yet another shelter. THAT was when she REALLY started to trust and obey me. I became *Mommy* and, though she still tested my rules, she conceded to the fact that it is *MOMMY'S house* and she wanted to live there.

Mommy's House isn't just a mean place full of rules and punishments though. Dakota LOVES music and has her own *playlist* that she listens to when she is crated. I downloaded some instrumental music from smooth-jazz and Native American artists onto an old cellphone. She especially likes music with wind instruments like piccolos and flutes. Her playlist also includes some *relaxation* music with wolves howling.

> Once, I even found her bopping her head, to the music, while she was lying quietly in her crate. She has come to love her music and becomes lethargic when I take it away as punishment. She, literally, becomes LISTless.

The TV show *Caesar 911* became her favorite show! As they say in the show's introduction, I did not try his advanced methods; but I did get a few tips and a whole lot of doggy behavioral understanding.

> When we played in the yard, instead of trying to keep her chained up, I took her off the chain and, fenced in a small area where she could move freely. As her behavior got better, the borders enlarged, and she earned more freedom in the yard. When she refused to obey, the perimeter shrunk back to its original size. She eventually realized that she preferred to run and play by my rules, in the two thousand and forty square-foot yard, instead of dominating HER eight-foot circle.

> Building her confidence was just as important. Little by little we started taking walks around the neighborhood. We started by walking to the corner daily; where she encountered traffic noises and learned to pass dogs, cats, squirrels, and ... (wait for it) ... people!

It took a while; but she learned to trust *Mommy* to protect her and began to ignore the distractions of her *natural enemies*. We have been able to extend our walks to an eight-block radius around our house.

When taking our walks, I tried several leashes and harness combinations until I found one that worked well with Dakota. I originally thought it was the STRENGTH of the leash that mattered; I was wrong. The leash we ended up using was probably the weakest of all the ones I tried.

I found that a "Nose Leash", with a short handle attached, in combination with a harness worked best for Dakota. Using traditional leashes that clicked to her collar or harness urged her pulling because her neck and chest are the most powerful parts of her body. Choke chains were absolutely out because she would seriously hurt herself before giving in! The nose leash allows me to *lead her by the nose* which is one of her more tender areas.

Koda, as I sometimes call her, seems to appreciate her living arrangements. She plays outside every morning, takes frequent walks, has a rotation of toys that keeps her from getting board, and eats a special diet of dog food mixed with canned vegetables (because of allergies).

She has a combination of doggy sweatshirts, jackets, and coats to keep her warm and dry in any weather. In addition, she has balloon-like boots that keep mud from squishing between her paws. Koda even has regular spa days where I *do her nails* and condition her paws.

A couple of times, recently, workmen left one of the backyard gates opened and Dakota realized it before I did. Both times, I found her idly nosing around right outside the fence. A year ago, I would have had to chase her to get her back into the yard. Nowadays, all I needed to do was call her back in, give her a welcome-home hug (like she gets after our neighborhood walks) and give her a treat. The first time I did this, she looked up at me as if to say, " I ain't goin' nowhere Mommy!"

Dakota was a REAL test. Truthfully, a good deal more than I was asking for; but I am glad I endured. Though she still tests me occasionally, she is a good dog, and I can tell she is happy with a Mommy that cares for and protects her.

If you have read all the previous stories, you may have already noticed the object lessons I just laid down. If not, here are a few:

- Beauty is only skin deep![45]

- God is the ultimate ALPHA.
  We try; but we cannot get in front of him[46]

- Trust your Heavenly Daddy; there is nothing to fear.[47]

- Jesus IS coming back... This place is not our home![48]

- The music you listen to is important.
  It CAN calm the troubled mind [49]

---

[45] Proverbs 31:30
[46] Revelation 1:8
[47] Jeremiah 29:11, Proverbs 3:5-6
[48] John 14:1-3
[49] I Samuel 16:23

- God can *enlarge our territory* [50] when we prove faithful in our current assignment.

- When we walk confidently lead by the Holy Spirit, we can overcome the anxieties of the world.[51]

- You can't "box with God", He's the LEADER of our Pack![52]

- Sometimes God keeps us "locked in" for no other reason than to let the fools pass by.[53]

- God leads His stiffed-necked people by their no's![54]

  (Pun intended.)

- God's promises have rewards and consequences attached.[55]

- Living by God's Standards make life easier here on earth [56]

- At times, OUR plans have microwave expectations while God is working at a crook-pot speed. His fundamental goal is always our salvation. By learning to endure, we get to see His wisdom (sometimes in hindsight) and reap the benefits of His highest plans for us.[57]

[50] I Chronicles 4:10
[51] I Corinthians 2:14
[52] II Chronicles 13:12
[53] Psalm 59:2-4, 9-10
[54] Exodus 33:5, II Kings 19:27-28
[55] Numbers 33:53, 55
[56] Psalm 119:173,175-176
[57] Ephesians 1:9-12

Raiders of the Lost Bark

2020

About four years ago, while daydreaming about the upcoming ten to twenty years, it dawned on me that I had not updated my plans. Tim and I had planned to move to the country and build two houses on shared acreage. Since Timothy was gone, I needed to revamp my plans for this imminent stage of life.

I kept my eyes, and mind, open for places I may want to live. The only thing, so far, that has become definite is that I want to live near my grandchildren.

When I first started downsizing, I was still waffling about keeping Dakota or finding her a new home. I was deciding whether I wanted a condo, rambler, or mobile home; which hobbies I wanted to continue or start; or in general, what lifestyle I wanted in these coming years?

Lately, I thought I was ready to move but I still had no idea where or what type of home I wanted. That is when I realized that I had not put the move before God.

I remembered that the process of moving INTO this house was preceded by much prayer. God had released me from my previous location (and situation) and blessed me with a home that met my every need, through several floorplans and even more life-event changes. Of course, I want Him to guide me into the NEXT stage.

So, I prayed, "God, you know my heart and you know my need. Please, let me know the plan." Sometime during the next night, or so, I had the following dream:

The dream started with me walking outside into the

backyard. My dog, Dakota, was in the process of digging a HUGE hole in my recently groomed lawn. I yelled for her to STOP!

I didn't actually SEE Dakota. She was presumably IN the hole; I was talking to her *presence.*

In anger, I turned around to go back into the house. I yelled over my shoulder, "Fill that hole back up!" When I got inside, I changed my mind and thought that the hole may come to serve a purpose as I tried to escape. So, I quickly ran back outside to tell Dakota, *Never mind and to leave the hole alone.* However, just that quickly when I returned outside, the hole looked filled-in.

I was thoroughly puzzled and told Dakota that I had planned to tell her to leave the hole alone. Nevertheless, before I finished my sentence, *Dakota*[58] pulled back a camouflage meshwork that revealed that she had not filled-in the hole. She snickered and said, "I knew you would change your mind."
I laughed and ran back into the house as if to get something.

A second later in a different scene, I watched myself, from an out-of-body view, dressed like Indiana Jones in *Raiders of the Lost Ark*. I was heading down some stairs leading into the hole Dakota had dug. The hole, though still in my backyard, had become more cave-like. Dakota, now a dog again, was going down the stairs beside me. As we walked, I

---

[58] At this point in my dream, *Dakota* was neither a dog nor a person. She was just a non-descript *presence.*

turned to her and said, "You're still temporary, you know!" Dakota, in a comedic rhythm, looked up at me and said in a jokingly, sarcastic Scooby-Do-growl, "Yeah, you're, rrrrright!"

I thought they were hilarious, they looked like a comedy team. As they headed down the stairs, I burst out in laughter when Dakota *killed-it* with:

Yeah, you're rrrright!

As I watched them, I laughed as I said, *Oh, what the adventure!*

I woke up and felt released.

I must admit, at that point, I was not sure if it was from God or my psyche. Either way, it was comically profound. Much more profound than I normally attribute to myself; therefore, I honestly believe God was speaking in HIS humorous way.

I do not usually remember my dreams so vividly. So, that alone meant a lot to me. Either way, in two quick scenes, decisions were made:

- I felt committed to the move.
- I had not noticed it before I heard the word *escape*;[59] but yes, I was in fact feeling somewhat *imprisoned*.
- I was keeping Dakota by my side, for now. She may or may not make it to the new house.
- I'll go *down* into the unknown because I know I am, now, ready to start the *adventure*.

---

[59] Specific verbiage is often important in my dreams.

The Corona; Vi -R- Us

It snuck up on us, "Like a thief in the night." The authorities knew about it in advance, but the general population did not have a clue. We were told it would be gone in a few weeks, yet it is still here with us a year later and, even now, we have just started to "turn the corner" to see what life after COVID-19 [60] may look like.

I am sure there will be hundreds of books written about Black Lives Matter, wearing masks (or not), George Floyd, Donald Trump, the COVID economy, the CDC, vaccines, and the many other ways this pandemic has changed the trajectory of the future. However, tracking world changing events is not my purpose. I simply want to testify as to how God leads me through this period.

It crossed my mind that the perfect political storm that allowed the corona germ to travel worldwide is just a glimpse of how God's last day prophecies CAN indeed come to be. [61]

My key thought remains:
Jesus masters political storms too! [62]

I am like a child holding my parent's hand in a crowded parade; trusting God to lead me through.

The COVID-19 pandemic hit the US in March of 2020. Most people, that were not classified as essential workers, *sheltered-in-place*. Because of that, many jobs shifted to work-from-home formats. Schools converted to online instruction and a

---

[60] the **CO**rona **VI**rus **D**isease 2019
[61] Revelation 16:2 ; Revelation 16
[62] Mark 4:39-41

new craze, called ZOOM, became a household word! The world was being run online; and almost everything was virtual. Even church services were held online and still all the more unique was the fact that senior citizens, that had earlier considered themselves computer illiterate, conquered the internet (or relied on their grandchildren) to reach out to their friends and family.

People everywhere started home projects to make use of their time during the pandemic's confinement. Following, is a walk through some of the projects that filled my time of isolation with productive pursuits.

❖ In March of 2018, a neighbor asked me to help her son with some schoolwork. Little did I know God was setting me up to help several other children also. In the days before COVID, I was having sessions in my living room. In March of 2020, indoor activities were discouraged so I took my tutorial sessions  from the living room to my front porch. Once I got my mosquito netting in place, the uniqueness of outdoor classes was a nice diversion for the kids. When winter of 2020 came, we joined the rest of the world online.

❖ Since the focus was on staying home and covid-safe, it came to mind to blend my love of the quiet of my *own back yard* with the thought of updating my landscaping. The yardwork kept me outside in the fresh air most of the Spring, Summer, and way into Fall before I completed it all, at which time the yard was indeed gorgeous!

❖ As Fall 2020 came and small outdoor gatherings were taking place, the yard became a charming backdrop for several small yard parties and front porch potlucks. These little get-togethers were ideal occasions to meet with friends and family for food, games, and outdoor relief  from the isolation we all had been enduring.

❖ When it became too cold to fellowship outside, my sisters and I started having weekly Zoom parties which, if truth be told, were our socialized excuses for silly games and computer-side snacks. By Thanksgiving, our *Thanksgiving Zoom Table* included framily from all across the USA. (North, South, East, AND West)

❖ While all this was going on, in the back of my mind, I was waiting for my previous publisher to finish processing this book.

Before the pandemic, they were scheduled to finish the book by December 2020. Because of COVID, they adjusted the schedule to February 2021. When we finally seemed ready to launch, the publisher vanished. [63]

In all honesty, this was perfect timing. It allowed me to extend the book from its previous ending (Destination Peace) to include the pandemic. I had been wanting to document SURVIVING the pandemic in Peace. So, amidst all the other projects, I decided to update and finish the book as well.

---

[63] Genesis 50:20

As the COVID lockdown extended into the winter, I added other projects. From the beginning, all the projects seemed to be a hodge-podge of activity and were just my way of trying to be productive. As time progressed, I saw the projects and life-events interlocking as if I had planned them. Here again, God was leading, and I did not realize it. Step by step he prepared me for "Life after Covid".

In mid-November 2020, as it got cooler outside, I moved my thoughts to indoor projects.

Note:

> *‣ I am giving more details for some of these activities because they may help someone else in their plans.*
> *‣ I am not necessarily recommending my choices. I am simply offering the details for informational purposes.*

❖ For several years I needed to revise my Will, Life Insurance Policies, and final wishes. Being stuck at home gave the perfect opportunity to finish pulling that information together and making modifications, updating documents, and registering my Will. I even mailed notebooks to both of my sons with copies of all the documents.

❖ In 2018 and 2019, I started to pursue a *Minimalist* [64] lifestyle. Being in isolation in the fall and winter of 2020 was the perfect time to revisit decluttering and downsizing my domestic footprint. I moved to the deeper stage of my decluttering.

> ‣ I initially started decluttering in the fall of 2019. I had boxes and shelves full of expensive figurines, vases, fine china, punch bowls, serving dishes, and other

---

[64] Minimalism – when a person deliberately chooses to live with only their basic necessities. Usually with the goal to reduce the clutter of stuff. The term minimalism is subjective; there is no set description and basic needs is a relative term.

paraphernalia. Not to mention the boxes and closets filled with leftovers from the boys' youth and the many *projects* of years gone by. Plus, I had several good quality paintings and pieces of artwork. I separated out the family heirlooms and the pieces I wanted to hold onto, and I was ready to sell (or trash) the rest.

> *They* say, "sell stuff on the internet" but the time and effort it takes to sell that many items did not seem worth it to me; I chose to organize a yard sale instead. I held a *Yard-Sale / Bar-b-que* and asked a few friends and family to help. Through the yard sale I reaped enough money to pay for the Bar-b-que, and the professional removal of the things that did not get sold or given to charitable organizations.

- In this stage of advanced decluttering, I shifted to my new décor and did a deeper cut. I kept a few pieces I TRULY enjoy, received some artwork from another downsizer (to refresh my decor), and shipped family treasures to their heirs and trustees. The rest was donated or tossed.

- No longer am I cluttering shelves with baubles, ornaments, and artifacts that just gather dust and causes more work.

- I'm learning to TALK about memories and save small mementos and pictures.

❖ The COVID-19 season also proved to be the perfect time to double check my financial wherewithal and updating my ten-year plan.

> *My mother, an accountant, taught me several principles of financial responsibility. Some she literally told me; others I learned by watching and listening.*

- Keep a simple budget.
- KNOW where your money is going.
- Live WITHIN your means
  - Money-out must not exceed money-in.
  - Do not charge items BECAUSE you do not have the cash. SAVE for it and then pay cash!
- Have an emergency fund.
- Have SAVINGS account(s).
- Only invest money you can afford to live without for several years.
- Build your credit score by paying the TOTAL balance on credit cards each month.
- A good credit rating can save you thousands of dollars in the long run.
- Use non-interest credit deals when available; but ONLY if you can pay the balance off BEFORE the expiration date.
- Be honest, with yourself, about NEEDs vs. wants.
- The only way to build generational wealth is to pass SOMETHING to your loved ones.
  - Don't PLAN to exhaust your finances.
  - Don't PLAN for your children to support you in your old age.
  - Life happens; but don't make THEM your plan A.
- Build multiple streams of income.
  - *aka* - always have at least one *side-hustle*.
- Real Estate is a good way to increase cash-flow.

I've been living by these rules for many years. Sometimes not totally adhering but always striving. I do wish I had had a little more time in Real Estate, but I had to come to grip with the fact that the pairing Timothy and I had was essential to our success.

Without him I am too soft-hearted; without me he would have been too harsh. Since I could not find a trustworthy partner to take his place, and my other sons were not interested, I had to give up real estate.

However, when the pandemic progressed and I heard about the moratorium put on covid related evictions, my inner landlord-ears perked up. I immediately knew that the post-covid real estate market would probably be extreme (either extremely good or extremely bad). I was sure it was going to be a defining moment in the market and I aimed to be ready for either.

❖ **Now**, in March 2021, the Pre-Post-Covid market IS crazy and the projects I completed earlier will be essential when responding as God continues to *guide me through this maze*!

At this point, the moratorium has not been lifted and there are very few houses available for sale. That makes a SELLER's market; a prime time to sell my house. I am ready with GREAT curb appeal and the house has been radically decluttered, therefore ready to *stage* and show.

❖ Back in February, when I began preparing for the move, I decided to use a Reverse Mortgage Loan to finance the new house.

The requirements of this type of loan HAS made the mechanics of the move a bit more challenging. Nonetheless, I believe it's the RIGHT choice— for me.

*Using a **Reverse Mortgage Loan** to PURCHASE a new home is a unique use of the loan. Why use it?*

➤ My sons are building lives in different states and DO NOT want to inherit a home where I plan to move.

- I am moving FROM a market where homes cost considerably less than the market I am moving INTO.
  - A RM loan increases my purchase power without creating a mortgage payment.
  - A RM loan means I will have money left over, from the equity of my old home, to combine with other assets.
- If there are any taxes generated in the transaction, this is probably my lowest earnings period because of COVID.
- PURCHASING with the RM loan keeps me from paying another set of *Closing* costs.
  - If I purchase with cash and THEN refinance with a RM loan, I'll pay for TWO *Closings*.
- The new home will be my final purchase.
  - My family will not inherit the unwelcomed task of selling it.
  - The mortgage company will manage selling it when I leave (either by death or moving).
  - My estate will receive any equity that may happen to be left after its sale.
  - AND one of the most important points in my estate planning:

    I am pulling the bulk of my equity NOW. It will go into my EMERGENCY fund and hopefully still be there to combine with life insurance in the inheritance I leave behind. However, it will be available to me if needed.

❖ My last project was planning the type of lifestyle I wanted for the upcoming ten years.

In my forties and fifties, while my income and body were strong enough to enjoy all kinds of activities, I purposely did most of my travelling.

I planned to live a quieter lifestyle in my sixties and seventies. A quieter, simpler lifestyle does not have to mean boring though. My next *shift* incorporates some of the things I am looking for in my new home. I look forward to an active *She-Shed,* possibly with a ceramics kiln. Also, my dollhouse furnishings were among the things I kept when downsizing and I look forward to building an encased dollhouse with working accessories like plumbing, lighting, wallpaper, and interior decorating. It will be part of my She-She Décor. Additionally, I look forward to establishing vegetable, fruit, and flower gardens, doing some more writing, and last but MOST of all, spending more time with the GRANDS!

This COVID period has been a sobering experience. For those of us trying to use the isolation in productive ways, it has been a time to RESET and SETUP things for the future. Seldom do we have the time to shift mindsets, finances, AND lifestyles. I count it a blessing to not just *survive* the pandemic, though that is a true blessing, but to REVIVE during the pandemic!

Steps to Faith

May **2021**

As we seem to approach the back end of the pandemic, my house HAS been listed for sale, we've (my agent and I) accepted an excellent offer and are stepping through the processes of Closing the sale.

Since I am still looking for my new home, I am planning to move into an apartment for the short interim. This feels strange to me; I have not lived in an apartment for over forty years.

I found several apartments with some of my needs. But, as hard as I looked for an appropriate apartment on the first floor, possibly with a balcony so I could sit outside in the fresh air, the only one availability that met all my other needs was a particular *BASEMENT* apartment.

- Its availability dates were right.
- It accepted dogs Dakota's size.
- It was in a familiar location, just up the street.
- It had good reviews online.
- The rent fit into my budget.
- I knew people that lived there.
 BUT… It is a *BASEMENT* apartment.
 AND…It does not even have a patio.

Not that there is anything sinister about basement apartments, I just did not want to LIVE underground with nothing but small windows for sunlight.

A few days later:
As I was talking to my sister Elena (from the story *King of the House*) about all the pros and cons, she framed the move as a step out on faith. The minute she said it, a flood of thoughts unfolded in a panoramic view.

God had already showed it to me, in my dream [65] depicted in the story *Raiders of the Lost Bark.*

> - There were STEPS going down into a hole.
>   *Symbolizing the stairs into the basement.*
> - The hole was in my backyard.
>   *Indicating - in my own backyard...*
>   *-or- a familiar, close-by location.*
> - I was dressed like Indiana Jones.
>   *Indicating - starting an adventure...*
>   *-or- expect the unexpected!*
> - The dream ENDED with Dakota and me walking down the steps and the future was not disclosed.
>   *Symbolizing - We were moving in FAITH.*

As usual: If I am listening,[66] -- HE PREPARES ME!

Later, I spoke about the dream and the circumstances with another one of my sisters, Jackie (from her quote *The Fifth Season*). She said, "It's like being a *Running Back* in a football game. In faith, you must get into position to RECEIVE the blessing God is about to send your way."

> My expanded thoughts (to myself) were:
> The *Running Back* must make sure to study the *Playbook* and know that the *COACH* is calling the plays. THEN, they can *run with all their might* to reach the *position*. If it is time to *receive*, they are ready. Otherwise, they can run interference for the *quarterback* as he advances the *ball.* [67]

---

[65] Isaiah 42:9; Daniel 2: 36
[66] Psalm 85:8
[67] Isaiah 40:31; Romans 8:28

So, I feel I am on the right path. God is asking for a willingness to go down those steps and start the adventure – in faith!

A few weeks later—

PS:

I accepted the apartment and gave the holding fee. We agreed that I would not sign a lease until the *Closing Date* was set for my home. However, because of complications, the closing date has been delayed. But guess what! That means I CAN move to a different apartment, one that isn't in the basement and maybe has a balcony; and the holding fee will apply to any new apartment. Like my sis said, I just needed to be in the *POSITION of acceptance* in order to move forward.

Finale'

For a good, LONG while I have been asking how and when this book would end.

God just answered:

*It started when you moved here (in faith) and finally learned to live in the provinces of **Peace**.*

*It ends with you leaving (in peace) learning to live in the refuge of **Faith**![68]*

Only God! Selah!

---

[68] Luke 7:50

Winnie's Pooh

2021

There are many personalities in the world. If people try to "pigeon-hole" me without getting to know me, they are usually wrong. They often take my quietness as being smug, shy, or aloof; many mistake my humility for stupidity and sometimes take my being sober as depressed, unexcitable, or drab. In general, I am not any of those.

> *On the contrary, I am usually quiet because I'm assessing. I am humble because I know God is my strength, and I am sober because I'm trying to control my impulsivity. Essentially, I am a problem solver at heart.*

As you have often seen in some of the previous stories, I have somber thoughts or predictions. They used to arouse anxiety until I reminded myself that foreseen endings CAN be revised by choices made along the way. [69] *I try to be aware of my spoken observations, but some people mistake discernment for divination. That is why I TRY to speak through my inner Pooh.*

During my career, in the Federal Government, I spent many years working as a Computer Network Engineer. My job descriptions usually included such duties as Network Administrator, LAN Technician, Systems Security Officer, Network Specialist, Telephone System Specialist, Help Desk Operator, User Training Coordinator, and Software Instructor.

> It was my job to be proactive; I was supposed to see trouble and execute solutions BEFORE the problems developed. I was a professional problem solver!

---

[69] Jonah 3:1- 4, 7-10

I wonder, which came first, the chicken or the egg? Did the jobs make me an Eeyore? Or did my Eeyore-ness equip me to do my duties well?

Whichever the case, I have noticed that I work well with the *Winnies* of the world. This crossed my mind recently when I thought about all the projects, potlucks, road trips, and even vacations I have taken with my *rag-tag* friends.

I have very few close friends and most of their personalities fall into distinct categories. There are two, maybe three, Pooh-Bears; a few Tiggers; and two or three Piglets. I have lost touch with both of my Rabbits. There is a Roo or two, a couple of Kangas, and then there are my wise Owls that speak wisdom into my life. My owls are not scatterbrained like the character in the book. They are my *best buds* when the *forest* gets dark and are usually the go-to pals that pull me back from the *rabbit-hole*.

Believe it or not, I cannot think of any other Eeyore-s in my life except my father and maybe Timothy. I guess the world can't handle a bunch of Eeyore-s hanging out together.

Wait a minute— Tim and my dad? Does that mean it is hereditary?

Oh No!! That explains a lot!

My friends are not one big group of friends, either. Many of them do not even know each other. However, I have learned that God has put these people in my path to help me find my way in the *forest*.

I think the reason we do so well is because we accept each other as we are. We laugh WITH each other about our weaknesses, and most of all, we LOVE each other despite them.

Note: When you recognize your pals, try to keep in touch with them; grow with them; laugh with them; cry with them. They make the journey FUN! [70]

To ALL my *forest pals,*
THANX!
You know who you are.

It has been a wonderful adventure!

.....
with miles to go before I sleep!
Frost ,1923

---

[70] GP are you with me?!

Scriptural References*

Introduction

Jeremiah 12:5	[5] If thou hast run with the footmen, and they have wearied thee, then how canst thou contend with horses? and if in the land of peace, wherein thou trustedst, they wearied thee, then how wilt thou do in the swelling of Jordan?
II Kings 6:16-17	[16] And he answered, Fear not: for they that be with us are more than they that be with them. [17] And Elisha prayed, and said, LORD, I pray thee, open his eyes, that he may see. And the LORD opened the eyes of the young man; and he saw: and, behold, the mountain was full of horses and chariots of fire round about Elisha

Journey to Canaan

Exodus 3:7 -8	[7] And the LORD said, I have surely seen the affliction of my people which are in Egypt, and have heard their cry by reason of their taskmasters; for I know their sorrows; [8] And I am come down to deliver them out of the hand of the Egyptians, and to bring them up out of that land unto a good land and a large, unto a land flowing with milk and honey; unto the place of the Canaanites, and the Hittites, and the Amorites, and the Perizzites, and the

*Unless otherwise noted,
all Bible quotations are taken from the KJV.

	Hivites, and the Jebusites.
Exodus 13:18	¹⁸ But God led the people about, through the way of the wilderness of the Red sea: and the children of Israel went up harnessed out of the land of Egypt.
Exodus 13:21-22	²¹ And the LORD went before them by day in a pillar of a cloud, to lead them the way; and by night in a pillar of fire, to give them light; to go by day and night: ²² He took not away the pillar of the cloud by day, nor the pillar of fire by night, from before the people.
Numbers 13:27–30	²⁷ And they told him, and said, We came unto the land whither thou sentest us, and surely it floweth with milk and honey; and this is the fruit of it. ²⁸ Nevertheless the people be strong that dwell in the land, and the cities are walled, and very great: and moreover we saw the children of Anak there. ²⁹ The Amalekites dwell in the land of the south: and the Hittites, and the Jebusites, and the Amorites, dwell in the mountains: and the Canaanites dwell by the sea, and by the coast of Jordan. ³⁰ And Caleb stilled the people before Moses, and said, Let us go up at once, and possess it; for we are well able to overcome it.

Even Dogs Get to Eat the Crumbs

Matthew 15:26-27	²⁶ But he answered and said, It is not meet to take the children's bread, and

	to cast it to dogs. ²⁷And she said, Truth, Lord: yet the dogs eat of the crumbs which fall from their masters' table.

The Master is Calling, Today!

Exodus 20:1–17	¹And God spake all these words, saying, ²I am the LORD thy God, which have brought thee out of the land of Egypt, out of the house of bondage. ³Thou shalt have no other gods before me. ⁴Thou shalt not make unto thee any graven image, or any likeness of any thing that is in heaven above, or that is in the earth beneath, or that is in the water under the earth. ⁵Thou shalt not bow down thyself to them, nor serve them: for I the LORD thy God am a jealous God, visiting the iniquity of the fathers upon the children unto the third and fourth generation of them that hate me; ⁶And shewing mercy unto thousands of them that love me, and keep my commandments. ⁷Thou shalt not take the name of the LORD thy God in vain; for the LORD will not hold him guiltless that taketh his name in vain. ⁸Remember the sabbath day, to keep it holy. ⁹Six days shalt thou labour, and do all thy work: ¹⁰But the seventh day is the sabbath of the LORD thy God: in it thou shalt not do any work, thou, nor thy son, nor thy daughter, thy manservant, nor thy maidservant, nor thy cattle,

	nor thy stranger that is within thy gates: [11] For in six days the LORD made heaven and earth, the sea, and all that in them is, and rested the seventh day: wherefore the LORD blessed the sabbath day, and hallowed it. [12] Honour thy father and thy mother: that thy days may be long upon the land which the LORD thy God giveth thee. [13] Thou shalt not kill. [14] Thou shalt not commit adultery. [15] Thou shalt not steal. [16] Thou shalt not bear false witness against thy neighbour. [17] Thou shalt not covet thy neighbour's house, thou shalt not covet thy neighbour's wife, nor his manservant, nor his maidservant, nor his ox, nor his ass, nor any thing that is thy neighbour's.
Psalm 100:3	[3] Know ye that the LORD he is God: it is he that hath made us, and not we ourselves; we are his people, and the sheep of his pasture.
Psalm 119:1	[119] Blessed are the undefiled in the way, who walk in the law of the LORD.
Matthew 25:21	[21] His lord said unto him, Well done, thou good and faithful servant: thou hast been faithful over a few things, I will make thee ruler over many things: enter thou into the joy of thy lord.
Psalm 100:4	[4] Enter into his gates with thanksgiving, and into his courts with praise: be thankful unto him,

	and bless his name.
Matthew 25:13	[13] Watch therefore, for ye know neither the day nor the hour wherein the Son of man cometh.

I come to the garden ....Alone?

John 15:4	[4] Abide in me, and I in you. As the branch cannot bear fruit of itself, except it abide in the vine; no more can ye, except ye abide in me.

Learning My Lessons Come First

Exodus 20:12	[12] Honour thy father and thy mother: that thy days may be long upon the land which the Lord thy God giveth thee.

2009 RECAP

Deuteronomy 11:19, 21	[19] And ye shall teach them [lessons] your children, speaking of them when thou sittest in thine house, and when thou walkest by the way, when thou liest down, and when thou risest up. [21] That your days may be multiplied, and the days of your children, in the land which the Lord sware unto your fathers to give them, as the days of heaven upon the earth.

Like A Needle to the Pole?

Romans 3:20	[20] Therefore by the deeds of the law there shall no flesh be justified in his sight: for by the law is the knowledge of sin.

| Romans 6:15 | [15] What then? shall we sin, because we are not under the law, but under grace? God forbid. |

If You Can't Stand the Heat,
Get Out of the Kitchen!

| Luke 10:38-42 | [38] Now it came to pass, as they went, that he entered into a certain village: and a certain woman named Martha received him into her house. [39] And she had a sister called Mary, which also sat at Jesus' feet, and heard his word. [40] But Martha was cumbered about much serving, and came to him, and said, Lord, dost thou not care that my sister hath left me to serve alone? bid her therefore that she help me. [41] And Jesus answered and said unto her, Martha, Martha, thou art careful and troubled about many things: [42] But one thing is needful: and Mary hath chosen that good part, which shall not be taken away from her. |
| John 4:13-14 | [13] Jesus answered and said unto her, Whosoever drinketh of this water shall thirst again: [14] But whosoever drinketh of the water that I shall give him shall never thirst; but the water that I shall give him shall be in him a well of water springing up into everlasting life. |

Walk Softly and Carry a Big Stick

| Exodus 14:21 | [21] And Moses stretched out his hand over the sea; and the LORD caused the sea to go back by a strong east wind |

	all that night, and made the sea dry land, and the waters were divided.

I Stand at the Door and Knock

Revelation 3:20	20 Behold, I stand at the door, and knock: if any man hear my voice, and open the door, I will come in to him, and will sup with him, and he with me.
Matthew 26:41	41 Watch and pray, that ye enter not into temptation: the spirit indeed is willing, but the flesh is weak.
Isaiah 6:8	8 Also I heard the voice of the Lord, saying, Whom shall I send, and who will go for us? Then said I, Here am I; send me
Philippians 3:13-14	13 Brethren, I count not myself to have apprehended: but this one thing I do, forgetting those things which are behind, and reaching forth unto those things which are before, 14 I press toward the mark for the prize of the high calling of God in Christ Jesus.
Mark 13:35-36	35 Watch ye therefore: for ye know not when the master of the house cometh, at even, or at midnight, or at the cockcrowing, or in the morning: 36 Lest coming suddenly he find you sleeping.
Matthew 13:6	6 And when the sun was up, they were scorched; and because they had no root, they withered away.

Mark 9:23-24	[23] Jesus said unto him, If thou canst believe, all things are possible to him that believeth.[24] And straightway the father of the child cried out, and said with tears, Lord, I believe; help thou mine unbelief.
Galatians 5:17	[17] For the flesh lusteth against the Spirit, and the Spirit against the flesh: and these are contrary the one to the other: so that ye cannot do the things that ye would.
Romans 7:15	[15] For that which I do I allow not: for what I would, that do I not; but what I hate, that do I.
Ephesians 3:20	[20] Now unto him that is able to do exceeding abundantly above all that we ask or think, according to the power that worketh in us,
Philippians 4:13	[13] I can do all things through Christ which strengtheneth me
Jude 24-25	[24] Now unto him that is able to keep you from falling, and to present you faultless before the presence of his glory with exceeding joy, [25] To the only wise God our Saviour, be glory and majesty, dominion and power, both now and ever. Amen

In Knowledge and Ammunition

I Corinthians 10:11	[11] Now all these things happened unto them for examples: and they are written for our admonition, upon whom the ends of the world are come.

Super-Fishial Love

Romans 12:4-5	4 For as we have many members in one body, and all members have not the same office: 5 So we, being many, are one body in Christ, and every one members one of another.
I Corinthians 10:13	13 There hath no temptation taken you but such as is common to man: but God is faithful, who will not suffer you to be tempted above that ye are able; but will with the temptation also make a way to escape, that ye may be able to bear it.
Mark 4:19	19 ... the cares of this world, and the deceitfulness of riches, and the lusts of other things entering in, choke the word, and it becometh unfruitful.
Matthew 6:31-33	31 Therefore take no thought, saying, What shall we eat? or, What shall we drink? or, Wherewithal shall we be clothed? 32 (For after all these things do the Gentiles seek:) for your heavenly Father knoweth that ye have need of all these things. 33 But seek ye first the kingdom of God, and his righteousness; and all these things shall be added unto you.
Ecclesiastes 3:1	1 To every thing there is a season, and a time to every purpose under the heaven:
Genesis 2:1-3	1 Thus the heavens and the earth were finished, and all the host of them. 2 And on the seventh day God ended

	his work which he had made; and he rested on the seventh day from all his work which he had made. [3] And God blessed the seventh day, and sanctified it: because that in it he had rested from all his work which God created and made.
Exodus 20:1-17	[1] And God spake all these words, saying, [2] I am the LORD thy God, which have brought thee out of the land of Egypt, out of the house of bondage. [3] Thou shalt have no other gods before me. [4] Thou shalt not make unto thee any graven image, or any likeness of any thing that is in heaven above, or that is in the earth beneath, or that is in the water under the earth. [5] Thou shalt not bow down thyself to them, nor serve them: for I the LORD thy God am a jealous God, visiting the iniquity of the fathers upon the children unto the third and fourth generation of them that hate me; [6] And shewing mercy unto thousands of them that love me, and keep my commandments. [7] Thou shalt not take the name of the LORD thy God in vain; for the LORD will not hold him guiltless that taketh his name in vain. [8] Remember the sabbath day, to keep it holy. [9] Six days shalt thou labour, and do all thy work: [10] But the seventh day is the sabbath of the LORD thy God: in it thou shalt not do any work, thou, nor thy son, nor thy daughter, thy manservant, nor thy maidservant, nor thy cattle, nor thy

	stranger that is within thy gates: [11] For in six days the LORD made heaven and earth, the sea, and all that in them is, and rested the seventh day: wherefore the LORD blessed the sabbath day, and hallowed it. [12] Honour thy father and thy mother: that thy days may be long upon the land which the LORD thy God giveth thee. [13] Thou shalt not kill. [14] Thou shalt not commit adultery. [15] Thou shalt not steal. [16] Thou shalt not bear false witness against thy neighbour. [17] Thou shalt not covet thy neighbour's house, thou shalt not covet thy neighbour's wife, nor his manservant, nor his maidservant, nor his ox, nor his ass, nor any thing that is thy neighbour's.
John 3:16	[16] For God so loved the world, that he gave his only begotten Son, that whosoever believeth in him should not perish, but have everlasting life.
Ephesians 6:10-14	[10] Finally, my brethren, be strong in the Lord, and in the power of his might. [11] Put on the whole armour of God, that ye may be able to stand against the wiles of the devil. [12] For we wrestle not against flesh and blood, but against principalities, against powers, against the rulers of the darkness of this world, against spiritual wickedness in high places. [13] Wherefore take unto you the whole armour of God, that ye may be able to withstand in the evil day, and having done all, to stand. [14] Stand

	therefore, having your loins girt about with truth, and having on the breastplate of righteousness;
Revelation 22:14	[14] Blessed are they that do his commandments, that they may have right to the tree of life, and may enter in through the gates into the city.
Revelation 22:20-21	[20] He which testifieth these things saith, Surely I come quickly. Amen. Even so, come, Lord Jesus. [21] The grace of our Lord Jesus Christ be with you all. Amen.
Matthew 4:19	[19] And he saith unto them, Follow me, and I will make you fishers of men.

A Nebuchadnezzar Moment

Daniel 2:31-37	[31] Thou, O king, sawest, and behold a great image. This great image, whose brightness was excellent, stood before thee; and the form thereof was terrible. [32] This image's head was of fine gold, his breast and his arms of silver, his belly and his thighs of brass, [33] His legs of iron, his feet part of iron and part of clay. [34] Thou sawest till that a stone was cut out without hands, which smote the image upon his feet that were of iron and clay, and brake them to pieces. [35] Then was the iron, the clay, the brass, the silver, and the gold, broken to pieces together, and became like the chaff of the summer threshingfloors; and the wind carried them away, that no place was found for them: and the stone that smote the

	image became a great mountain, and filled the whole earth. ³⁶ This is the dream; and we will tell the interpretation thereof before the king. ³⁷ Thou, O king, art a king of kings: for the God of heaven hath given thee a kingdom, power, and strength, and glory.
Daniel 2:36-43	³⁶ This is the dream; and we will tell the interpretation thereof before the king. ³⁷ Thou, O king, art a king of kings: for the God of heaven hath given thee a kingdom, power, and strength, and glory. ³⁸ And wheresoever the children of men dwell, the beasts of the field and the fowls of the heaven hath he given into thine hand, and hath made thee ruler over them all. Thou art this head of gold. ³⁹ And after thee shall arise another kingdom inferior to thee, and another third kingdom of brass, which shall bear rule over all the earth. ⁴⁰ And the fourth kingdom shall be strong as iron: forasmuch as iron breaketh in pieces and subdueth all things: and as iron that breaketh all these, shall it break in pieces and bruise. ⁴¹ And whereas thou sawest the feet and toes, part of potters' clay, and part of iron, the kingdom shall be divided; but there shall be in it of the strength of the iron, forasmuch as thou sawest the iron mixed with miry clay. ⁴² And as the toes of the feet were part of iron, and part of clay, so the kingdom shall be partly strong, and partly broken. ⁴³ And

	whereas thou sawest iron mixed with miry clay, they shall mingle themselves with the seed of men: but they shall not cleave one to another, even as iron is not mixed with clay.
Daniel 4:30-34	[30] The king spake, and said, Is not this great Babylon, that I have built for the house of the kingdom by the might of my power, and for the honour of my majesty? [31] While the word was in the king's mouth, there fell a voice from heaven, saying, O king Nebuchadnezzar, to thee it is spoken; The kingdom is departed from thee. [32] And they shall drive thee from men, and thy dwelling shall be with the beasts of the field: they shall make thee to eat grass as oxen, and seven times shall pass over thee, until thou know that the most High ruleth in the kingdom of men, and giveth it to whomsoever he will. [33] The same hour was the thing fulfilled upon Nebuchadnezzar: and he was driven from men, and did eat grass as oxen, and his body was wet with the dew of heaven, till his hairs were grown like eagles' feathers, and his nails like birds' claws. [34] And at the end of the days I Nebuchadnezzar lifted up mine eyes unto heaven, and mine understanding returned unto me, and I blessed the most High, and I praised and honoured him that liveth for ever, whose dominion is an everlasting dominion, and his kingdom is from

	generation to generation:
Exodus 6:1-3	[1] Then the LORD said unto Moses, Now shalt thou see what I will do to Pharaoh: for with a strong hand shall he let them go, and with a strong hand shall he drive them out of his land. [2] And God spake unto Moses, and said unto him, I am the LORD: [3] And I appeared unto Abraham, unto Isaac, and unto Jacob, by the name of God Almighty, but by my name JEHOVAH was I not known to them.
Daniel 4:37	[37] Now I Nebuchadnezzar praise and extol and honour the King of heaven, all whose works are truth, and his ways judgment: and those that walk in pride he is able to abase.
Daniel 3:14-18	[14] Nebuchadnezzar spake and said unto them, Is it true, O Shadrach, Meshach, and Abednego, do not ye serve my gods, nor worship the golden image which I have set up? [15] Now if ye be ready that at what time ye hear the sound of the cornet, flute, harp, sackbut, psaltery, and dulcimer, and all kinds of musick, ye fall down and worship the image which I have made; well: but if ye worship not, ye shall be cast the same hour into the midst of a burning fiery furnace; and who is that God that shall deliver you out of my hands? [16] Shadrach, Meshach, and Abednego, answered and said to the king, O Nebuchadnezzar, we are not careful to answer thee in this matter.

	¹⁷ If it be so, our God whom we serve is able to deliver us from the burning fiery furnace, and he will deliver us out of thine hand, O king. ¹⁸ But if not, be it known unto thee, O king, that we will not serve thy gods, nor worship the golden image which thou hast set up.
Daniel 3:21	²¹ Then these men were bound in their coats, their hosen, and their hats, and their other garments, and were cast into the midst of the burning fiery furnace.
Daniel 3:24-25	²⁴ Then Nebuchadnezzar the king was astonished, and rose up in haste, and spake, and said unto his counsellors, Did not we cast three men bound into the midst of the fire? They answered and said unto the king, True, O king. ²⁵ He answered and said, Lo, I see four men loose, walking in the midst of the fire, and they have no hurt; and the form of the fourth is like the Son of God.
Malachi 3:10	¹⁰ Bring ye all the tithes into the storehouse, that there may be meat in mine house, and prove me now herewith, saith the LORD of hosts, if I will not open you the windows of heaven, and pour you out a blessing, that there shall not be room enough to receive it.
Luke 6:38	³⁸ Give, and it shall be given unto you; good measure, pressed down, and shaken together, and running over,

	shall men give into your bosom. For with the same measure that ye mete withal it shall be measured to you again.
Philippians 1:6	[6] Being confident of this very thing, that he which hath begun a good work in you will perform it until the day of Jesus Christ:
Luke 12:48	[48] But he that knew not, and did commit things worthy of stripes, shall be beaten with few stripes. For unto whomsoever much is given, of him shall be much required: and to whom men have committed much, of him they will ask the more.
Psalms 23:1-4	[1] The LORD is my shepherd; I shall not want. [2] He maketh me to lie down in green pastures: he leadeth me beside the still waters. [3] He restoreth my soul: he leadeth me in the paths of righteousness for his name's sake. [4] Yea, though I walk through the valley of the shadow of death, I will fear no evil: for thou art with me; thy rod and thy staff they comfort me. [5] Thou preparest a table before me in the presence of mine enemies: thou anointest my head with oil; my cup runneth over. [6] Surely goodness and mercy shall follow me all the days of my life: and I will dwell in the house of the LORD for ever
Genesis 37:8	[8] And his brethren said to him, Shalt thou indeed reign over us? or shalt thou indeed have dominion over us?

	And they hated him yet the more for his dreams, and for his words.
Genesis 37:23-28	23 And it came to pass, when Joseph was come unto his brethren, that they stript Joseph out of his coat, his coat of many colours that was on him; 24 And they took him, and cast him into a pit: and the pit was empty, there was no water in it. 25 And they sat down to eat bread: and they lifted up their eyes and looked, and, behold, a company of Ishmeelites came from Gilead with their camels bearing spicery and balm and myrrh, going to carry it down to Egypt. 26 And Judah said unto his brethren, What profit is it if we slay our brother, and conceal his blood? 27 Come, and let us sell him to the Ishmeelites, and let not our hand be upon him; for he is our brother and our flesh. And his brethren were content. 28 Then there passed by Midianites merchantmen; and they drew and lifted up Joseph out of the pit, and sold Joseph to the Ishmeelites for twenty pieces of silver: and they brought Joseph into Egypt.
Romans 8:31	31 What shall we then say to these things? If God be for us, who can be against us?
Daniel 4:30-32; 34	30 The king spake, and said, Is not this great Babylon, that I have built for the house of the kingdom by the might of my power, and for the honour of my majesty? 31 While the word was in the king's mouth, there fell a voice from

	heaven, saying, O king Nebuchadnezzar, to thee it is spoken; The kingdom is departed from thee. ³² And they shall drive thee from men, and thy dwelling shall be with the beasts of the field: they shall make thee to eat grass as oxen, and seven times shall pass over thee, until thou know that the most High ruleth in the kingdom of men, and giveth it to whomsoever he will. ³⁴ And at the end of the days I Nebuchadnezzar lifted up mine eyes unto heaven, and mine understanding returned unto me, and I blessed the most High, and I praised and honoured him that liveth for ever, whose dominion is an everlasting dominion, and his kingdom is from generation to generation:
John 19:30	³⁰ When Jesus therefore had received the vinegar, he said, It is finished: and he bowed his head, and gave up the ghost.

The Gospel of the Hedges

Ecclesiastes 9:5	⁵ For the living know that they shall die: but the dead know not any thing, neither have they any more a reward; for the memory of them is forgotten.
Revelation 20:13–14	¹³ And the sea gave up the dead which were in it; and death and hell delivered up the dead which were in them: and they were judged every man according to their works. ¹⁴ And death and hell

	were cast into the lake of fire. This is the second death.

TOO MUCH STUFF!

Matthew 11:28–29	28 Come unto me, all ye that labour and are heavy laden, and I will give you rest. 29 Take my yoke upon you, and learn of me; for I am meek and lowly in heart: and ye shall find rest unto your souls.

Maintenance

Philippians 4:13	13 I can do all things through Christ which strengtheneth me.

Handle It!

III John 1:2 {Health}	2 Beloved, I wish above all things that thou mayest prosper and be in health, even as thy soul prospereth.
Luke 16:10–13 {Finances}	10 He that is faithful in that which is least is faithful also in much: and he that is unjust in the least is unjust also in much. 11 If therefore ye have not been faithful in the unrighteous mammon, who will commit to your trust the true riches? 12 And if ye have not been faithful in that which is another man's, who shall give you that which is your own? 13 No servant can serve two masters: for either he will hate the one, and love the other; or else he will hold to the one, and despise the other. Ye cannot serve God and mammon.

Ecclesiastes 9:10, 12 {Time}	[10] Whatsoever thy hand findeth to do, do it with thy might; for there is no work, nor device, nor knowledge, nor wisdom, in the grave, whither thou goest. [12] For man also knoweth not his time: as the fishes that are taken in an evil net, and as the birds that are caught in the snare; so are the sons of men snared in an evil time, when it falleth suddenly upon them.
John 3:16–17 {Salvation}	[16] For God so loved the world, that he gave his only begotten Son, that whosoever believeth in him should not perish, but have everlasting life. [17] For God sent not his Son into the world to condemn the world; but that the world through him might be saved.
I Peter 3:3–4 {Clothing}	[3] … let it not be that outward adorning of plaiting the hair, and of wearing of gold, or of putting on of apparel; [4] But let it be the hidden man of the heart, in that which is not corruptible, even the ornament of a meek and quiet spirit, which is in the sight of God of great price.
I Corinthians 6:18–20 {Sexuality}	[18] Flee fornication. Every sin that a man doeth is without the body; but he that committeth fornication sinneth against his own body. [19] What? know ye not that your body is the temple of the Holy Ghost which is in you, which ye have of God, and ye are not your own? [20] For ye are bought with a price: therefore glorify God in your body,

	and in your spirit, which are God's.
II Corinthians 5:17 {Sexuality}	¹⁷ Therefore if any man be in Christ, he is a new creature: old things are passed away; behold, all things are become new.

Do You Still Believe in Santa?

Matthew 10:30-33	³⁰ But the very hairs of your head are all numbered. ³¹ Fear ye not therefore, ye are of more value than many sparrows. ³² Whosoever therefore shall confess me before men, him will I confess also before my Father which is in heaven. ³³ But whosoever shall deny me before men, him will I also deny before my Father which is in heaven.

Life Cycles

John 11:11–14	¹¹ These things said he: and after that he saith unto them, Our friend Lazarus sleepeth; but I go, that I may awake him out of sleep. ¹² Then said his disciples, Lord, if he sleep, he shall do well. ¹³ Howbeit Jesus spake of his death: but they thought that he had spoken of taking of rest in sleep. ¹⁴ Then said Jesus unto them plainly, Lazarus is dead.
I Thessalonians 4:16	¹⁶ For the Lord himself shall descend from heaven with a shout, with the voice of the archangel, and with the trump of God: and the dead in Christ shall rise first:
I Kings 17:8-10	⁸And the word of the Lord came unto him [Elijah], saying, ⁹ Arise, get thee

	to Zarephath, which belongeth to Zidon, and dwell there: behold, I have commanded a widow woman there to sustain thee [during the famine]. [10] So he arose and went to Zarephath. And when he came to the gate of the city, behold, the widow woman was there gathering of sticks: and he called to her, and said, Fetch me, I pray thee, a little water in a vessel, that I may drink. [God blessed Elijah, the widow, and her son for three years]
Psalm 23:4-5, 6	4 Yea, though I walk through the valley of the shadow of death, I will fear no evil: for thou art with me; thy rod and thy staff they comfort me. [5] Thou preparest a table before me in the presence of mine enemies: thou anointest my head with oil; my cup runneth over. [6] Surely goodness and mercy shall follow me all the days of my life: and I will dwell in the house of the Lord for ever.

Be Fruitful and Multiply

Matthew 13:23	[23] But he that received seed into the good ground is he that heareth the word, and understandeth it; which also beareth fruit, and bringeth forth, some an hundredfold, some sixty, some thirty.
Job 42:12-13	[12] So the Lord blessed the later end of

	Job more than his beginning: for he had fourteen thousand sheep, and six thousand camels, and a thousand yoke of oxen, and a thousand she asses. [13] He had also seven sons and three daughters.

The FIFTH Season

Leviticus 26:3-4	[3] If ye walk in my statutes, and keep my commandments, and do them; [4] Then I will give you rain in due season, and the land shall yield her increase, and the trees of the field shall yield their fruit.
Luke 12:42-44	[42] And the Lord said, Who then is that faithful and wise steward, whom his lord shall make ruler over his household, to give them their portion of meat in due season? [43] Blessed is that servant, whom his lord when he cometh shall find so doing [44] Of a truth I say unto you, that he will make him ruler over all that he hath.
Galatians 6:9	[9] And let us not be weary in well doing: for in due season we shall reap, if we faint not.

Color to the Edge of the Page

I Corinthians 10: 31	[31] Whether therefore ye eat, or drink, or whatsoever ye do, do all to the glory of God.

Follow the Leader

Judges 2:10	[10] And also all that generation were

	gathered unto their fathers: and there arose another generation after them, which knew not the LORD, nor yet the works which he had done for Israel.

My Life's Story is My Sacrifice

Psalm 40: 6–8	⁶ Sacrifice and offering thou didst not desire; mine ears hast thou opened: burnt offering and sin offering hast thou not required. ⁷ Then said I, Lo, I come: in the volume of the book it is written of me, ⁸ I delight to do thy will, O my God: yea, thy law is within my heart.
Deuteronomy 30:11–12, 14	¹¹ For this commandment which I command thee this day, it is not hidden from thee, neither is it far off. ¹² It is not in heaven, that thou shouldest say, Who shall go up for us to heaven, and bring it unto us, that we may hear it, and do it? ¹⁴ But the word is very nigh unto thee, in thy mouth, and in thy heart, that thou mayest do it.
Luke 14:21–24	²¹ So that servant came, and shewed his lord these things. Then the master of the house being angry said to his servant, Go out quickly into the streets and lanes of the city, and bring in hither the poor, and the maimed, and the halt, and the blind. ²² And the servant said, Lord, it is done as thou hast commanded, and yet there is room. ²³ And the lord said unto the servant, Go out into the highways and hedges, and compel them to come in,

	that my house may be filled. ²⁴ For I say unto you, That none of those men which were bidden shall taste of my supper.
Matthew 25:3-10	³ They that were foolish took their lamps, and took no oil with them: ⁴ But the wise took oil in their vessels with their lamps. ⁵ While the bridegroom tarried, they all slumbered and slept. ⁶ And at midnight there was a cry made, Behold, the bridegroom cometh; go ye out to meet him. ⁷ Then all those virgins arose, and trimmed their lamps. ⁸ And the foolish said unto the wise, Give us of your oil; for our lamps are gone out. ⁹ But the wise answered, saying, Not so; lest there be not enough for us and you: but go ye rather to them that sell, and buy for yourselves. ¹⁰ And while they went to buy, the bridegroom came; and they that were ready went in with him to the marriage: and the door was shut.
Luke 17:4	⁴ And if he trespass against thee seven times in a day, and seven times in a day turn again to thee, saying, I repent; thou shalt forgive him.
Acts 2:38	³⁸ Then Peter said unto them, Repent, and be baptized every one of you in the name of Jesus Christ for the remission of sins, and ye shall receive the gift of the Holy Ghost.
II Samuel 23:2	² The Spirit of the LORD spake by me, and his word was in my tongue.

Malachi 4:1-3	[1] For, behold, the day cometh, that shall burn as an oven; and all the proud, yea, and all that do wickedly, shall be stubble: and the day that cometh shall burn them up, saith the LORD of hosts, that it shall leave them neither root nor branch. [2] But unto you that fear my name shall the Sun of righteousness arise with healing in his wings; and ye shall go forth, and grow up as calves of the stall. [3] And ye shall tread down the wicked; for they shall be ashes under the soles of your feet in the day that I shall do this, saith the LORD of hosts.
Luke 12:30–34	[30] For all these things do the nations of the world seek after: and your Father knoweth that ye have need of these things. [31] But rather seek ye the kingdom of God; and all these things shall be added unto you. [32] Fear not, little flock; for it is your Father's good pleasure to give you the kingdom. [33] Sell that ye have, and give alms; provide yourselves bags which wax not old, a treasure in the heavens that faileth not, where no thief approacheth, neither moth corrupteth. [34] For where your treasure is, there will your heart be also.
I Kings 11:4	[4] For it came to pass, when Solomon was old, that his wives turned away his heart after other gods: and his heart was not perfect with the LORD his God, as was the heart of David his father.

Destination---*Peace*

Ecclesiastes 4:6	[6] Better is an handful with quietness, than both the hands full with travail and vexation of spirit.
Proverbs 15:16	[16] Better is little with the fear of the LORD than great treasure and trouble therewith.
Hebrews 11:16	[16] But now they desire a better country, that is, an heavenly: wherefore God is not ashamed to be called their God: for he hath prepared for them a city.
Isaiah 26:3	[3] Thou wilt keep him in perfect peace, whose mind is stayed on thee: because he trusteth in thee.

2020 Hindsight

Psalm 37:23	[23] The steps of a good man are ordered by the Lord: and he delighteth in his way.

Dakota's in the house

Proverbs 31:30	[30] Favour is deceitful, and beauty is vain: but a woman that feareth the Lord, she shall be praised.
Revelation 1:8	[8] I am Alpha and Omega, the beginning and the ending, saith the Lord, which is, and which was, and which is to come, the Almighty.
Jeremiah 29:11	[11] For I know the thoughts that I think toward you, saith the Lord, thoughts of peace, and not of evil, to give you an expected end.

Proverbs 3:5-6	[5] Trust in the Lord with all thine heart; and lean not unto thine own understanding. [6] In all thy ways acknowledge him, and he shall direct thy paths.
John 14:1-3	[1] Let not your heart be troubled: ye believe in God, believe also in me. [2] In my Father's house are many mansions: if it were not so, I would have told you. I go to prepare a place for you. [3] And if I go and prepare a place for you, I will come again, and receive you unto myself; that where I am, there ye may be also.
I Samuel 16:23	[23] And it came to pass, when the evil spirit from God was upon Saul, that David took an harp, and played with his hand: so Saul was refreshed, and was well, and the evil spirit departed from him.
I Chronicles 4:10	[10] And Jabez called on the God of Israel, saying, Oh that thou wouldest bless me indeed, and enlarge my coast, and that thine hand might be with me, and that thou wouldest keep me from evil, that it may not grieve me! And God granted him that which he requested.
I Corinthians 2:14	[14] But the natural man receiveth not the things of the Spirit of God: for they are foolishness unto him: neither can he know them, because they are spiritually discerned.
II Chronicles 13:12	[12] And, behold, God himself is with us for our captain, and his priests with

	sounding trumpets to cry alarm against you. O children of Israel, fight ye not against the Lord God of your fathers; for ye shall not prosper.
Psalm 59:2-4, 9-10	[2] Deliver me from the workers of iniquity, and save me from bloody men. [3] For, lo, they lie in wait for my soul: the mighty are gathered against me; not for my transgression, nor for my sin, O Lord. [4] They run and prepare themselves without my fault: awake to help me, and behold. [9] Because of his strength will I wait upon thee: for God is my defence. [10] The God of my mercy shall prevent me: God shall let me see my desire upon mine enemies.
Exodus 33:5	5 For the Lord had said unto Moses, Say unto the children of Israel, Ye are a stiffnecked people: I will come up into the midst of thee in a moment, and consume thee: therefore now put off thy ornaments from thee, that I may know what to do unto thee.
II Kings 19:27-28	27 But I know thy abode, and thy going out, and thy coming in, and thy rage against me. 28 Because thy rage against me and thy tumult is come up into mine ears, therefore I will put my hook in thy nose, and my bridle in thy lips, and I will turn thee back by the way by which thou camest.
Numbers 33:53, 55	53 And ye shall dispossess the inhabitants of the land, and dwell therein: for I have given you the land

	to possess it.
	55 But if ye will not drive out the inhabitants of the land from before you; then it shall come to pass, that those which ye let remain of them shall be pricks in your eyes, and thorns in your sides, and shall vex you in the land wherein ye dwell.
Psalm 119:173, 175-176	173 Let thine hand help me; for I have chosen thy precepts. 175 Let my soul live, and it shall praise thee; and let thy judgments help me. 176 I have gone astray like a lost sheep; seek thy servant; for I do not forget thy commandments.
Ephesians 1:9-12	9 Having made known unto us the mystery of his will, according to his good pleasure which he hath purposed in himself: 10 That in the dispensation of the fulness of times he might gather together in one all things in Christ, both which are in heaven, and which are on earth; even in him: 11 In whom also we have obtained an inheritance, being predestinated according to the purpose of him who worketh all things after the counsel of his own will: 12 That we should be to the praise of his glory, who first trusted in Christ.

The Corona Vi -R- us

Revelation 16	1 And I heard a great voice out of the temple saying to the seven angels, Go your ways, and pour out the vials of the wrath of God upon the earth.

² And the first went, and poured out his vial upon the earth; and there fell a noisome and grievous sore upon the men which had the mark of the beast, and upon them which worshipped his image. ³ And the second angel poured out his vial upon the sea; and it became as the blood of a dead man: and every living soul died in the sea. ⁴ And the third angel poured out his vial upon the rivers and fountains of waters; and they became blood. ⁵ And I heard the angel of the waters say, Thou art righteous, O Lord, which art, and wast, and shalt be, because thou hast judged thus. ⁶ For they have shed the blood of saints and prophets, and thou hast given them blood to drink; for they are worthy. ⁷ And I heard another out of the altar say, Even so, Lord God Almighty, true and righteous are thy judgments. ⁸ And the fourth angel poured out his vial upon the sun; and power was given unto him to scorch men with fire. ⁹ And men were scorched with great heat, and blasphemed the name of God, which hath power over these plagues: and they repented not to give him glory. ¹⁰ And the fifth angel poured out his vial upon the seat of the beast; and his kingdom was full of darkness; and they gnawed their tongues for pain, ¹¹ And blasphemed the God of heaven because of their pains and their sores, and repented not of their deeds. ¹² And the sixth angel poured out his vial upon the

great river Euphrates; and the water thereof was dried up, that the way of the kings of the east might be prepared. [13] And I saw three unclean spirits like frogs come out of the mouth of the dragon, and out of the mouth of the beast, and out of the mouth of the false prophet.[14] For they are the spirits of devils, working miracles, which go forth unto the kings of the earth and of the whole world, to gather them to the battle of that great day of God Almighty. [15] Behold, I come as a thief. Blessed is he that watcheth, and keepeth his garments, lest he walk naked, and they see his shame. [16] And he gathered them together into a place called in the Hebrew tongue Armageddon. [17] And the seventh angel poured out his vial into the air; and there came a great voice out of the temple of heaven, from the throne, saying, It is done. [18] And there were voices, and thunders, and lightnings; and there was a great earthquake, such as was not since men were upon the earth, so mighty an earthquake, and so great. [19] And the great city was divided into three parts, and the cities of the nations fell: and great Babylon came in remembrance before God, to give unto her the cup of the wine of the fierceness of his wrath. [20] And every island fled away, and the mountains were not found. [21] And there fell upon men a great hail out of heaven, every

	stone about the weight of a talent: and men blasphemed God because of the plague of the hail; for the plague thereof was exceeding great.
Mark 4:39-41	[39] And he (Jesus) arose, and rebuked the wind, and said unto the sea, Peace, be still. And the wind ceased, and there was a great calm. [40] And he said unto them, Why are ye so fearful? How is it that ye have no faith? [41] And they feared exceedingly, and said one to another, What manner of man is this, that even the wind and the sea obey him?
Genesis 50:20	[20] But as for you, ye thought evil against me; but God meant it unto good, to bring to pass, as it is this day, to save much people alive.

Steps to Faith

Isaiah 42:9	[9] Behold, the former things are come to pass, and new things do I declare: before they spring forth I tell you of them.
Daniel 2: 36	[36] This is the dream; and we will tell the interpretation thereof before the king.
Psalm 85:8	[8] I will hear what God the Lord will speak: for he will speak peace unto his people, and to his saints: but let them not turn again to folly.
Isaiah 40:31	[31] But they that wait upon the Lord shall renew their strength; they shall mount up with wings as

	eagles; they shall run, and not be weary; and they shall walk, and not faint.
Romans 8:28	[28] And we know that all things work together for good to them that love God, to them who are the called according to his purpose.

Finale'

Luke 7:50	And he said to the woman, Thy faith hath saved thee; go in peace.

Winnie's Pooh

Jonah 3:1-4, 7-10	[1] And the word of the LORD came unto Jonah the second time, saying, [2] Arise, go unto Nineveh, that great city, and preach unto it the preaching that I bid thee. [4] And Jonah began to enter into the city a day's journey, and he cried, and said, Yet forty days, and Nineveh shall be overthrown. [7] And he [Nineveh's King] caused it to be proclaimed and published through Nineveh by the decree of the king and his nobles, saying, Let neither man nor beast, herd nor flock, taste any thing: let them not feed, nor drink water: [8] But let man and beast be covered with sackcloth, and cry mightily unto God: yea, let them turn every one from his evil way, and from the violence that is in their hands. [9] Who can tell if God will turn and repent, and turn away from his

fierce anger, that we perish not? [10] And God saw their works, that they turned from their evil way; and God repented of the evil, that he had said that he would do unto them; and he did it not.

Bibliography

Bertino, Sergio. 604447, Photo. Available: Dreamstime.com 2011

Birtic, Tomislav. 236845, Photo. Available: Dreamstime.com 2011

Caraman, ©. SantaWithTools,photo.Available: Dreamstime.com 2011

Choudhuryl, MohammedAnwarul. 15577807, Photo. Available: Dreamstime.com 2010

Collodi, Carlo. *Pinochio*. Danny Kaye and Sandy Duncan, 1976 TV Musical

Cynoclub. 14855471, Photo. Available: Dreamstime.com 2010

Cynoclub. 16985401, Photo. Available: Dreamstime.com 2009

Cynoclub. 2195949, Photo. Available: Dreamstime.com 2011

Darkleaf. 195534460, Photo. Available: Dreamstime.com 2021

D'Avella, M. *Minamalism*.Joshua Fields Millburn and Ryan Nicodemus, 2016 Netflix Documentary

Do, LeThuy. 11196330, Photo. Available: Dreamstime.com 2009

Frost, Robert. *Stopping by Woods on a Snowy Evening*, 1923 Poem

Isselee. 12911746, Photo. Available:
Dreamstime.com 2011

Isselee. 18989709, Photo. Available:
Dreamstime.com 2011

Justinen, Lars. "We Will not Bow Down",
Photo. Available:Goodsalt.com 2008

Kentannenbaum. 5645020, Photo. Available:
Dreamstime.com 2011

Lee, Stan/ Kirby, Jack. *The Incredible
Hulk.* Marvel Comics, 1962, Dayton

Mathayward. 18984531, Photo. Available:
Dreamstime.com 2011

Nezhinskii,Sergei. 92248311, Photo. Available:
Dreamstime.com 2021

Nezhinskii,Sergei. 92248324, Photo. Available:
Dreamstime.com 2021

Nezhinskii,Sergei. 138674161, Photo. Available:
Dreamstime.com 2021

Patty, Sandi. *We Shall Behold Him.*
Love Overflowing, 1981

Preve,Beatrice. 14771424, Photo. Available:
Dreamstime.com 2011

Raphael, Douglas. 4377095, Photo.
Available: Dreamstime.com 2011

Rogul ,Nikita. 490487, Photo. Available:
Dreamstime.com 2011

Rozum. 13547261, Photo. Available:
Dreamstime.com 2011

Silberschuh9875. 5207705, Photo.
Available: Dreamstime.com 2011

Snap Inc. Pam and Dakota, Bitmoji.
Created: Bitmoji.com 2021

Stangot. 18148118, Photo. Available:
Dreamstime.com 2011

Stanica, Tudor. 1082547, Photo. Available:
Dreamstime.com 2006

Spielberg.S.*Raiders of the Lost Ark*. Harrison
Ford and Karen Allen, 1982, Paramount Pictures

The Brooklyn Tabernacle Choir.
More Than Enough. God is Working (Live),
TuneCore/SME, 2000

Tindley, Charles. Beams of Heaven.
New Songs of Paradise, No.6, 1916

Tourtellott Matthew. 51426, Photo.
Available: Dreamstime.com 2011

Walker, Hesekiah. I Need You to Survive.
Family Affair II Live at Radio City Music Hall,
2002

Zhang, Hongqi. 14540234, Photo. Available:
Dreamstime.com 2010

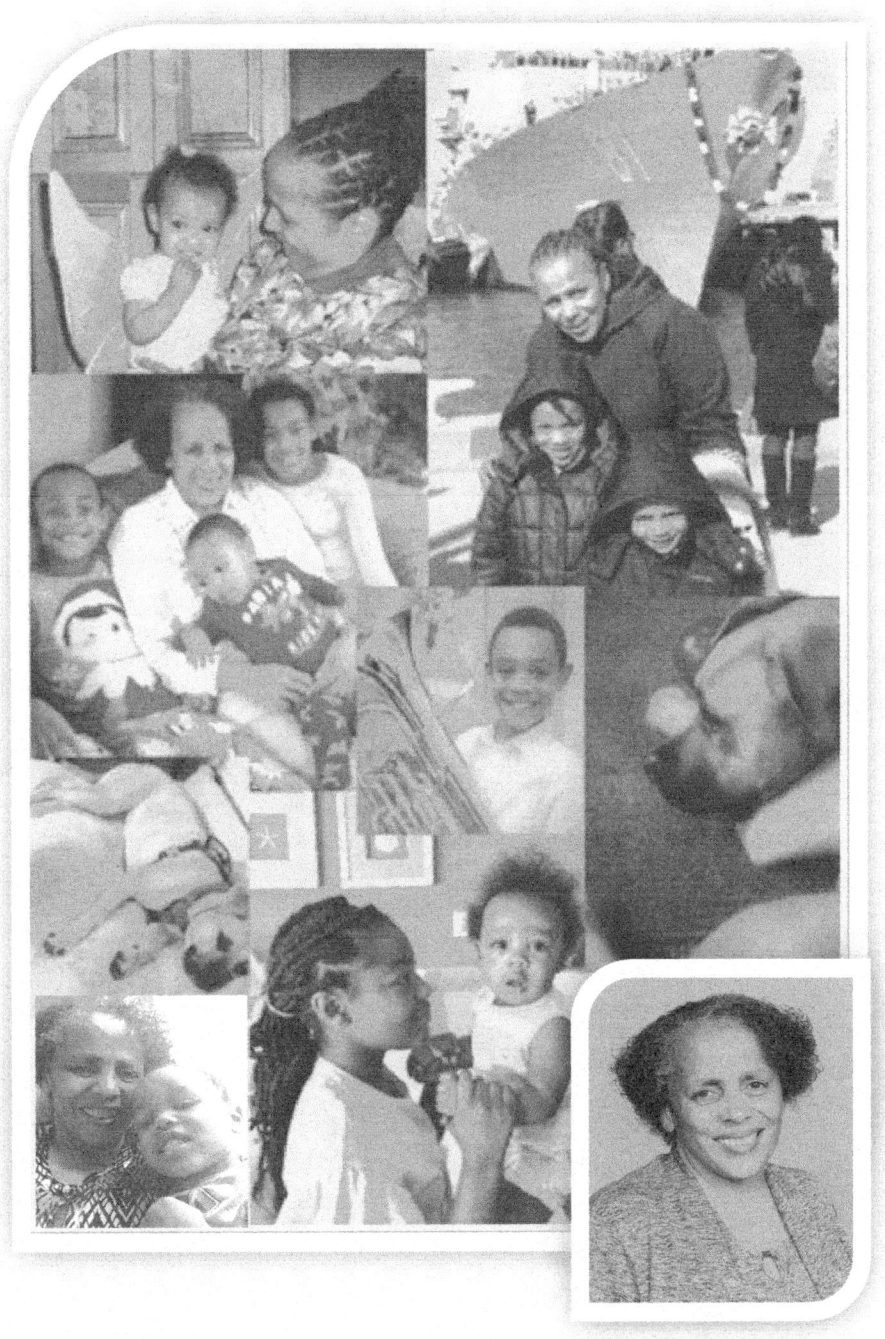